Business and Politics

A comparative introduction

Business and Politics

A comparative introduction

Graham K. Wilson

University of Wisconsin - Madison

CHATHAM HOUSE PUBLISHERS, INC.
Chatham, New Jersey

338.91

W 748

BUSINESS AND POLITICS

© Graham K. Wilson 1985

Published in the United States of America by
CHATHAM HOUSE PUBLISHERS INC.
Box One, Chatham, New Jersey 07928

ISBN 0-934540-51-9 (cloth)
ISBN 0-934540-50-0

Printed in Hong Kong

10 9 8 7 6 5 4 3 2 1

To my wife, Virginia Sapiro

Contents

Preface

One of the few by-products of the economic difficulties which have afflicted the world in the 1970s and 1980s is a revival of interest in political economy. The central place of discussion of the performance of economies in political debate has encouraged many to ask again some of the basic questions about the relationship between government and the economy. Does government dominate business, or does business dominate government? Is the relationship between business and government effectively structured so that such widely shared goals as economic growth and full employment are likely to be attained, or not? How do business and government interact?

Although the relationship between business and government now forms part of almost all university courses on individual political systems, the topic is rarely studied *comparatively*. Courses on the comparative study of legislatures, executives and political parties are far more common than courses which compare the relationship between government and business, in spite of the importance and popularity of the topic. It is my belief, which I hope the following book will substantiate, that there is at least as much variation in the business–government relationship as there is in the character of political parties. Failure to appreciate the variation in this relationship from country to country may result in practical disadvantages for those who wish to make their careers in business; it also enfeebles debate within individual countries about the nature of their own political economy. Failure to appreciate the unique aspects of one's own system leads in political economy – as in the study of political institutions and practices – to an unnecessarily shallow understanding of it; a comparative approach is the only remedy.

Any attempt to cover as broad a range of countries as concisely as I have attempted in this book is to run a high risk of writing a book which the experts on individual countries will find in their own area to be shallow and incomplete. I hope that they will accept my apologies for trespassing outside my own usual specialisms. I have taught courses on business and politics for several years now in both Britain and the USA, and have been aware of the lack of a short book which would provide students with some picture of the range of relationships between business and government found in the capitalist, industrialised democracies. I have attempted to fill that gap with this book, and hope that the range of countries covered will compensate for my failure to provide more extensive detail on each. As those used to planning long car journeys will know, there are advantages to both detailed and more comprehensive maps. I hope the Bibliography of this book will provide some assistance to students who wish to obtain more detailed 'maps' of the topics covered in outline here.

Inevitably, portions of such a general work as this rest on my reading of secondary sources. I am deeply indebted to the Nuffield Foundation, however, for their generous support in conducting research on aspects of the relationship between business and government which has informed many sections of this book. I am also profoundly grateful for the intellectual companionship of Virginia Sapiro during the writing of this book.

GRAHAM K. WILSON

1

Introduction

The Business–Government Relationship

The relationship between business and government has emerged as one of the central issues of contemporary politics. The questions raised by political scientists, commentators and citizens about this relationship vary considerably, however. For some people, the question is whether the relationship between business and government is such that basic economic objectives are likely to be achieved. This raises at its simplest questions about the government's record. Is unemployment higher or lower than when the government came to power? Are real incomes increasing or falling? Are prices steady or increasing?

More reflective commentators have asked whether the structure of the relationship between business and government – as opposed to day-to-day events – serves in the long term to promote or to hinder the attainment of such shared economic objectives. This raises questions such as whether the relationship between business and government is structured in such a way as to minimise the risk that government will adopt policies which will inadvertly hurt business activity – for example, increasing costs or decreasing competitiveness when policy alternatives without these disadvantages were available and acceptable. Is government kept aware of the needs of industry and commerce in the making of policy in matters as important to them as transport, education, and the promotion of science and technology? Is, in short, business sufficiently effective in expressing its concerns to government to warn government when its essential purposes may be endangered? We may summarise these concerns by asking whether or not the relationship between government and business is *efficient* in promoting the achievement of objectives (such as higher employment and increased living standards) which need not divide business and government.

The agreement which exists in most quarters on the desirability of economic growth does not mean that there is anything approaching general agreement on the means of attaining that growth, or on the particular relationship between government and industry which will best promote it. Anyone who has heard arguments in a pub or train on this subject, or who followed the 1983 British General Election, will be aware of the chasm which separates the believer in detailed government intervention in the economy (through planning or even public ownership) from those who believe that – at least in economic matters – government is best which governs least, leaving business as free as possible to cope with market forces. Government intervention is seen as necessary by some to counter clear failings of market mechanisms; to others, government intervention is a disruptive interference with otherwise efficient market mechanisms.

In contrast to these questions of efficiency are the questions of *distribution* raised by political scientists and commentators. A wide variety of books have been written arguing that business has extensive and, by implication, excessive power. Some of these arguments are based on the analyses of particular policies or the links between politicians and business executives. Defence contractors in the USA,[1] major oil companies in a variety of countries,[2] car manufacturers in Britain and the USA, shipyards, steel mills and aircraft manufacturers more or less round the world have all been accused of 'feeding at the public trough', extorting unfair assistance from government. Others have argued that employment, tax, consumer and environmental laws reflect the power of business. A wide variety of mechanisms have been adduced to explain this alleged dominance of government by business. The shared background of business executives and top officials in government,[3] the contributions which business executives or their companies make to the electoral campaigns of politicians,[4] the number and skill of lobbyists employed by business concerns to put across their case, and the sensitivity of politicians to the votes of those employed in the relevant concerns are all advanced in both political science and popular debate as reasons for the power of business in democratic political systems. The question of whether there is a power élite which links (presumably to the disadvantage of the public) top government officials and business executives has been much discussed in relation to both Britain and the USA.[5] Probably the most sweeping of the distributive theories of business–government relations are those in the Marxist tradition. There are a great variety of such Marxist theories, however, partly because Marx himself did not develop an explicit theory of the relationship between state and capital.[6] Marxist theories themselves vary tremendously – particularly in terms of the role they ascribe to ideology, and to the degree to which the state is bound to follow the dictates of capital, or is the site itself of fights between labour, capital, or even 'fractions' of capital and labour trying to shape public policy.

Ideally, the political scientist would cast a dispassionate light on these questions. Unfortunately, there are a variety of reasons why it is particularly difficult to gather evidence or assemble arguments on these issues. Take, for example, the questions of *efficiency* which we have already examined. It is reasonably easy to compile satisfactory statistics which should show levels of economic growth, employment, and changes in real income or prices in different countries. There is also increasing knowledge of the patterns of relationships which prevail between business and government in different countries. Attempts to link economic performance in a particular country to the nature of the business–government relationship will however, encounter, objections that the real explanation for a country's economic success or failure are to be found in other factors such as the culture of the country, its unions, the quality of its management, etc. It may even be argued plausibly that emulating the business–government relationship in a different country without adopting its culture and society will make matters worse. It might be that attempts by Britain or the USA to emulate the Japanese pattern of government–industry relations would thus only exacerbate their economic problems, in spite of the apparent success of that relationship in Japan.

Even more severe problems await those who try to assess the political power of business through studying systematically the *distributive* questions. At the heart of these disputes is the lack of consensus in political science about the meaning of 'power' – and particularly about the importance of its more directly observable aspects compared with other less visible dimensions.

The most widely accepted form of power is the form emphasised by pluralist political scientists. A has power over B to the extent that B behaves in a manner which B would not have done without A's intervention. In principle, though there could be major practical difficulties in securing access to the relevant information, the exercise and the extent of power can be observed. The original intentions of A and B can be ascertained, as well as the nature of their dealings. The extent of A's 'victory' can be ascertained and – if the dealings are continuous – the frequency of A's victory can be assessed.[7]

The pluralist concept of power has been subject to sustained criticism now for over twenty years. Many of these criticisms are particularly relevant to the study of business and politics. The first criticism made was that the pluralist measure of power is of value only when there is an observable clash of interests or opinions. In some situations, one interest may be so powerful that issues are not raised and potential views or interests are not expressed in the political system.[8] Crenson has argued that the power of US Steel in Gary, Indiana was so extensive that the issue of controlling the pollution from its furnaces was not raised.[9] Crenson argues that the people of Gary probably wanted clean air, but did not dare raise the issue because US Steel had such a dominance of the town that to do so would have been futile or costly. Similarly, it is beyond doubt that business is well aware of the importance of public opinion. Television viewers in Britain and the USA are treated to commercials showing heroic oil company workers struggling with the freezing temperatures of Alaska or the waves of the North Sea to bring the public its petrol or heating oil. Other commercials show the care taken by the oil companies to protect the environment. To the extent that public opinion is willing (or is persuaded) to take a favourable view of business, business has acquired a valuable political resource. It was probably the case that many Americans in the 1950s would have shared the view attributed to a member of President Eisenhower's Cabinet, Secretary of Defence Charles Wilson, that 'what is good for General Motors is good for the United States'. Public trust in the integrity of business executives, and belief that business executives tried to strike a fair balance between the public interest and profit, were high. It was unlikely, therefore, that there would be determined efforts to impose on business policies unwelcome to it, for such policies would have little popularity. A major observable clash of interests between business and government or business and other interests groups would be unlikely to occur because the climate of opinion was so favourable to business.

The critics of pluralism have proposed other measures of power to take account of the problems they have raised. Crenson borrowed the concept of 'non-decision' or a 'second face of power' from its originators, Bachrach and Baratz. The second face of power was the power to protect one's interests through the exclusion from political discussion or the policy agenda proposals which could be damaging to them. In Gary, proposals to require US Steel to spend large sums on preventing pollution were thus excluded from the political agenda and were not even seriously discussed.

Steven Lukes[10] argued that to take account of the climate of opinion – or what in Marxist terms might be called the 'dominant ideology' – it was necessarily to acknowledge a third face of power: the power to shape opinion in such a way that people with conflicting interests were unable to formulate a challenge to the dominant interest. Those believing that what was good for General Motors was always good for them would not even be able fully to imagine, let alone support, policies unwelcome to General Motors.

Other writers have stressed the importance of *structural* aspects of the power of business. Business leaders, writers such as Lindblom[11] have stressed, are not just another interest group analogous to the League Against Cruel Sports or an anti-abortion movement. On the contrary, business leaders in market societies dispose of real power because they have been entrusted with the power to decide whether (and where) to invest in the new processes which are vital to the future prosperity of the whole community. If business leaders feel that the conditions are not right for investment, if business confidence is lacking, then that investment will not be made – or, more probably, will be made elsewhere. In Europe governments thus compete for the international car companies such as Ford to build new plants in their country and not in a rival one; in the USA the states compete with each other to attract industry by having the lowest corporation taxes and in other ways creating a 'favourable business environment'. Business executives can consult league tables which rank each US state in terms of its 'business climate'.

Most of these theories have an obvious value and plausibility in supplementing the pluralist analysis of the power of business. They are also, however, subject to serious criticisms. Both the second and third faces of power theories are open to the objection that the observer using them is imposing his or her own values on the people in the situation being studied. To say (following Bachrach and Baratz) that a particular proposal should have been discussed – and the fact that it was not indicates the power of those whose interest would have been hurt by the proposal – seems to involve making a judgement that the proposal was of such obvious value and importance that its neglect needs explanation; it is always possible that those involved in the situation might not agree. Lukes's third face of power theory similarly involves asserting that people who have absorbed a pro-business ideology have a form of 'false consciousness' which blinds them to their true interests. Only those confronted with particularly bizarre ideologies (such as an argument from a poor white in the old deep South of the USA that he had common interests with plantation owners) or those such as Marxists who ascribe to an over-arching theory of society and human nature will be happy making such assertions. Most social scientists would be wary of imposing readily their own values on the subjects of their study.

Crenson's attempt to avoid this problem illustrates how severe the problem is. Crenson argued that we could assume that the desire to avoid pollution – which is damaging to the health – is so universal that failure to propose pollution controls could be a sign only of domination by a hostile interest. Further reflection indicates that this is not necessarily so. People living in Gary – particularly if they were working for US Steel – might believe that if the company was not bothered with pollution controls and their expense, it could pay higher wages, invest more and create new jobs, and at least would refrain from locating elsewhere. This would be true particularly if – and there seems to have been some evidence that this was the case – the population of Gary consisted of people attracted by hopes of high wages, who perhaps planned to stay in the town for only a limited time. Such considerations could rationally lead them not to favour pollution control laws.

Lindblom's argument that business has structural power can be similarly criticised, in spite of its plausibility. If business executives decide not to carry out an investment because the political climate is not right, they pay a price; potential profits are foregone. Even decisions about where to locate a factory or other plant cannot be made in response simply to the political climate in the planned location. A copper company may be forced to open a copper mine in Chile even if it fears expropriation by a left-wing government, because there is no other source of copper so readily available from a mining point of view. Closing a factory and transferring its production to a new plant in a low-wage, low-cost environment may be very costly in the short term, and such things as markets or the supply of raw material may also exert a more powerful effect on location than differences in government policy. Moreover, the needs of business in relation to government are neither as homogeneous nor as simple as we have so far supposed. Some businesses, such as textiles, need a comparatively unskilled, low-wage workforce and as few government regulations and as low taxes as possible. The computer industry has very different needs. A skilled, highly-educated workforce is sufficiently important that it is better to locate in a country or state with good educational system than one with low taxes and a poor educational system. (The American microchip industry is a case in point, locating in California and Massachusetts, not the South.) High government spending and taxation may provide businesses with benefits as diverse as lively cultural centres (of value in attracting top executives and their families to the area), or a good road system. Politicians are likely to be given a surprisingly wide-ranging 'shopping list' by companies whom they solicit, and such apparently obvious demands as low taxation may not, in fact, figure very prominently. A survey of business executives in the USA in 1983 suggested that low company taxation was listed as only the thirteenth most important factor in deciding where to locate a new plant.

In spite of the difficulties which each of these theories creates, few would deny that each contributes to a fuller understanding of the power of business. It is also obviously the case that the importance of these factors will vary considerably from country to country. It might be plausible to argue that a dominant, pro-business ideology dominates thinking in the USA, inhibiting fundamental challenges to capitalism; the question 'Why is there no socialism in the United States?' has been debated at least since Sombart wrote the classic book of that name.[12] It is surely less plausible to argue that a dominant ideology precludes challenges to business in countries such as Italy or France where Communist and Socialist parties have received a major proportion of the votes cast in elections. Less obviously, it is almost certainly the case that attitudes to business fluctuate *within* each country over time. In the USA, for

example, the high levels of trust in business executives common in
the 1950s gave way by the 1970s to high levels of distrust and
scepticism, recovering somewhat in the 1980s. Similarly (as we shall
see) the degree to which business is organised to take part in politics
in pluralist fashion through lobbying, campaign contributions, etc.
varies very significantly over time. It is probably wise, therefore, to
think of the different theories of the power of business not as
permanently mutually exclusive theories, but as descriptions of factors
which may vary in importance from country to country, and from
period to period within the same country, in determining the power
of business.

Types of Policy and Organisation of Business

Bauer, Pool and Dexter published in 1962 a study of American
business and public policy which was one of the most carefully
researched books on any aspect of American politics till then
published.[13] We shall have cause to refer to this book in detail later;
it also prompted one of the most influential book reviews in political
science. The reviewer, Theodore Lowi, took Bauer, Pool and Dexter
to task for basing a book on American business and public policy
on a single topic: tariff policy. Lowi argued that policies shape the
pattern of politics associated with them. In particular, there were
three major types of policy which shaped the pattern of politics.[14]
These were *distributive* policies (such as tariffs, government contracts,
etc., *redistributive* policies (such as progressive taxation and welfare
policies), and *regulatory* policies (such as the imposition of rules
concerning pollution by government on industry). In each of these
types of policy, Lowi contended that the same interest (such as
business) would find itself in a different web of political relationships
and dealings.

The adequacy of Lowi's typology and the question of how to
define the types of policy in practice need not detain us here. We
should note, however, that Lowi is undoubtedly correct in his claim
that different policy areas will involve business in different types of
politics. There will obviously be a difference between the politics of
issues which divide industry and the politics of issues which unite
it. When it comes to exerting political pressure to win a defence
contract, the situation is obviously one in which it is every firm for

itself. In the USA, for example, such aircraft builders as Lockheed and Boeing have waged mighty battles, involving newspaper campaigns and the Representatives and Senators from areas where the firms' factories are located, in the quest for military contracts. There are, however, issues which unite business. Issues such as the level of corporation tax affect all companies. Regulations to limit the exposure of workers to noise considered by the Health and Safety Commission in Britain, would affect so many firms (and practically all engaged in manufacturing) that again there can be a common front on the issue. Some issues (such as the level of rates) are a matter of concern to both very large and very small businesses, whereas other issues (such as exchange rate policy) affect primarily only medium-sized and large concerns.

The frequency with which issues which unite rather than divide business arise varies from country to country. In general we should expect that this in turn will affect the character of business organisations. Where issues affecting all businesses are raised frequently, business may be expected to create more impressive organisations to raise common interests than in countries where such issues are rare. A strong socialist or union movement would therefore be likely to be accompanied by a strong employers' organisation. Countries in which socialism (or a similar general challenge to business interests) and unions were both weak would be unlikely to have a strong central employers' organisation. As we shall see, there is considerable evidence to support these propositions. The central employers' organisations of Britain, Germany and Sweden are much more impressive organisations than the employers' organisations of the USA, where both unions and radical challenges to capitalism have been comparatively weak. The degree to which the small business owner is willing to throw in his or her lot with the multinational enterprise in paying membership dues to an organisation purporting to represent both depends to a major degree on the extent to which both feel that they have important (but threatened) common interests.

Many other factors help shape the character of business organisation. The political cultures of Western democracies differ considerably in the degree to which they bestow legitimacy on the representation of views and interests through interest-group activity as opposed to through political parties, legislators and other elected politicians. In some countries close, confidential discussions between interest group officials and government officials are regarded as part of everyday life; in other countries such gatherings are regarded as potential conspiracies, so that a public record of such meetings and their purpose is required.

The character of government itself also contributes to these differences. In parliamentary systems characterised by tight party discipline and a small number of parties, governments can control the access of interest groups to key decision-makers. Policy is decided in secret and, in effect, ratified by the legislature under a system of tight party discipline. If an interest group is to have a substantial impact on policy, it must ensure that it is consulted early in the development of policy. Once policy is announced publicly, it will be hard to press a government to change policy, particularly as that might be seen as involving a loss of face. Yet access to ministers or civil servants in the formative stages of policy may be limited to groups which in some way or other satisfy ministers and civil servants.

Apart from expecting groups to be responsible in their policies ministers in such a system will also try to encourage sectors such as farming, business and unions to designate a single group as its spokesman. Such a designation saves ministers or civil servants the awkward task of aggregating interests within as well as between sectors. It is generally embarrassing for politicians to be confronted with two or more groups disagreeing about what their members, drawn from the same economic sector, actually want. Politicians, therefore, may well try to limit effective access to one group per sector, when they have the chance to do so. In systems characterised by fragmentation in government – whether through a separation of powers or through a fragmented party system – such restrictions in access are difficult to enforce. If a group in the USA finds that it is not welcome at the White House, it may well find that it is welcome at the equally important Congressional committee which is handling the subject. Attempts by politicians to cajole American business interest groups into a single body comparable to the Confederation of British Industries (CBI) in Britain or the Austrian employers' organisation are unlikely to succeed.

A further influence on the character of employers' organisations is the nature of labour relations and bargaining in the system. Obviously, a collective bargaining system in which the unit of bargaining is an industry rather than the firm is likely to encourage the development of strong *trade associations* representing all the employers within that industry. Once an employers' association has developed with the primary purpose of representing employers within an industry in wage negotiations, it is a comparatively simple matter for the organisation to take on the role of representing that industry to government. Many matters of public policy are sufficiently technical, too, that the trade association is a more useful form of representation than a body speaking for all employers. There will, moreover, always be issues in any political system which tend to set one sector against another. Oil companies can be expected to favour policies raising the price of oil; companies using that oil to manufacture products such as artificial fibres are likely to be less enthusiastic. There is a high probability that if an organisation trying to speak for all employers is confronted with such a disagreement, it will respond by doing nothing. To take either side would be to risk irritating important members, perhaps even causing them to disaffiliate from the organisation. The threat of disaffiliation is a powerful one in employers' organisations, and whenever a split between employers in different industries or large firms emerges, inaction is the most likely outcome for the general employers' organisation. The trade association then comes into its own. There are also occasions when the general employers' organisation is unwilling to align itself too closely with a particular industry because of political or image factors. Asbestos companies, for example, have such a poor image today in most countries that the general, comprehensive employers' organisation is unwilling to associate employers as a whole with the cause of asbestos companies. Again, the trade association comes into its own.

The nature of employers' political representation is affected finally by the degree of industrial concentration – the extent to which production is concentrated in the hands of a very few companies. When companies become very large, it is possible for them to afford, without inconvenience, their own representation. One of the clearest trends in the USA in recent years has been for individual firms to become much more actively and openly involved in politics. Individual companies, as well as trade associations, collect money to give to the campaigns of Congressional candidates, and employ their own representatives in Washington to liaise with the Executive branch agencies and Congressional committees of particular importance to the firm. Such representation can be a supplement to

membership of a trade association or a general employers' organisation. It can also be of value when there is no consensus within an
industry on the government policies desired. Thus the US car
industry has been quite sharply divided on the extent to which it
wants the USA to have a more protectionist trade policy; General
Motors is much less interested in protection than are Ford or
Chrysler. Individual representation for a company is even more
important when it comes to exerting political pressure for government contracts, where companies inevitably bid against each other.

Political scientists have become increasingly aware in recent years
of the contrasts between Western democracies in the extent to which
relatively unified organisations speaking for broad economic sectors –
such as farmers, employers or unions – are influential in shaping public
policy. In some countries, the relationship between government, the
national employers' organisation and the national union federation
is so close and important that the political systems have been labelled
corporatist (or, to avoid pejorative connotations, neo-corporatist).[15]
In such systems, important aspects of public policy are made after
consultations approximating to negotiations between government
and 'monopolistic' interest groups with the exclusive right to represent
employers and unions. Government generally plays an active role in
shaping economic development through plans for the economy as
a whole or individual sectors, and through advancing money and
providing protection behind trade barriers to industries which are
thought to have a promising future. Incomes policies may well be
settled in such tripartite dealings, too, so that the division of national
income between business, labour and government is settled in
negotiations between them. Crucial to the definition of corporatist or
neo-corporatist systems, however, is that they should be systems in
which the economic interests speaking for employers or unions should
have a high degree of *influence* (compared with explicitly political
actors, such as legislators) in the shaping of government policy.
Governments turn as easily to the leaders of employers' organisations
or the unions and perhaps more frequently than they turn to legislators
or parties for advice, permission and approval in undertaking major
policy changes.

Political systems are not corporatist or non-corporatist in absolute
terms. The degree to which political systems are corporatist varies
along a spectrum ranging from a situation in which they are not at
all corporatist to one in which they are totally corporatist, only

economic interest groups having any influence over government, and all major decisions being made in dealings between government and these groups. There are also countries which have some industrial sectors which are more corporatist than others, and countries which are 'imperfectly' corporatist in that only employers (and not unions) are taken into partnership with government so that, because of the weakness of labour, the partnership is two-, not three-sided. We should not assume either that employers in a more corporatist system are more advantaged than employers in a less corporatist one. Employers in a country characterised by corporatist relations between business, labour and government may well be in such a relationship precisely because they have a more powerful challenge to cope with from unions or governments ready to 'interfere' with business than employers in a country not classifiable as corporatist. Corporatist patterns of policy-making may also oblige employers to forgo certain political strategies, or to play down their involvement in electoral poltics as the price of partnership with business or labour.

Nevertheless, the degree to which government–industry relations can be considered corporatist provides a valuable perspective for a comparative book such as this. In some of the Western democracies which we shall examine, the relationship between government and industry has been very close and highly institutionalised; Sweden and Austria are the obvious examples. In other countries, notably the USA, the relationship between government and industry is very loosely institutionalised, though there are obviously many personal links between politicians and business executives. Although party politics and elections in Sweden and Austria are important, they can be considered as being towards the corporatist end of the spectrum of the countries covered in this book. Although the USA is not without any trace of corporatism (the defence industries being fairly close to having a corporatist relationship with government), we can with confidence place the USA towards the opposite end of the spectrum. France will be seen to have greater similarities to the Japanese in that government has institutionalised ties to government (but not labour), while the British are more like the Americans in not fully institutionalising such ties. We shall see that in order of increasing corporatism the countries coverd in the text can be ranked: the USA, Germany, Britain, France, Japan, Sweden and Austria.

Business and Electoral Politics

Our concern so far has been very much with the activities of business interest groups. Business does indeed operate as a business group, but its political activities are much broader than that. In most political systems there is one party which is closely associated with business; the party receives the preponderance of the votes of managers, shareholders, etc., and raises a significant proportion of its funds from contributions from business. The Republican Party in the USA, the Liberal Party in Japan, and the Conservative Party in Great Britain obviously fall in this category.[16]

The norms governing relationships between business and the pro-business party differ, however. In the USA, for example, it is illegal for companies to make political contributions out of their general funds. This situation (which has existed legally since 1926, though enforced effectively only since 1974) contrasts with the situation in Britain, where companies have openly and legally supplied the Conservative Party with a large proportion (until recently, a major-ity) of its funds from their general accounts. The Japanese case is analogous to that in Britain. The managers and shareholders of large companies obviously constitute (except through subscriptions to insurance policies and pension plans) a minority of the population. It is rarely wise for a political party to be indentified too closely, therefore, as the party of business. The price of electoral victory is likely to be a need to put some distance between the party and business.

As we have noted above, business is not a homogeneous unit. At least three differences in types of business are likely to have political relevance. These are differences between financial institutions (such as banks, insurance companies and other investing institutions), manufacturing and mining firms, and small businesses (ranging from restaurants to garages). In Britain, obvious differences have arisen between financial institutions and manufacturing firms. High interest rates and a high value for sterling have worked to the advantage of financial institutions, labelled 'the City'. High interest rates have brought high incomes for the City institutions, and the high value of sterling prevailing in the early 1980s made investment overseas, a long-standing strategy of the City, an easier option than would otherwise have been the case. In the USA, differences between very large institutions (both financial and manufacturing) on the one hand, and small-scale business ('Main Street') have long been noted in the degree to which unions and social expenditure on welfare, food stamps and health care have been tolerated. Though the entire business community in America opposed such policies at their inception, most big business – referred to sometimes as Wall Street and sometimes as the East Coast Establishment – has been more willing to tolerate their continuance than has 'Main Street'.

It is of some importance, therefore, to go beyond the labelling of a party as 'pro-business' and to ask what section (or, as it is sometimes called in rather ugly terminology, 'fraction') of the business community is dominant within the party in question. The balance of power within the parties obviously fluctuates. The British Conservative Party has become more dominated by people connected with finance and less dominated by landowners than in the past. The rise of President Reagan within the American Republican Party has been linked to the decline in power of the East Coast Establishment (including Wall Street) and the rise of Western entrepreneurs whose current attitudes are closer to 'Main Street' than to Wall Street. Throughout the post-Second World War era, however, relatively small-scale, locally-orientated business people have had more influence in the USA than in Britain. The individualised entrepreneurial campaigning style of candidates for the House of Representatives and Senate have made local élites considerably more important politically than in Britain or Japan.

In contrast to both Britain and Japan, conservative politics in France, Germany and the USA also has a religious dimension with which economic interests of business must be accommodated. This is perhaps most obvious in the USA where the moral concerns of the 'Moral Majority' (although it is, in fact, neither a majority nor particularly moral) coexist with most business concerns without trouble. Banning abortion or 'dirty' books does not cause serious problems for Exxon, while the 'Moral Majority' causes may lure some votes away from liberal Democrats likely to be perceived by business executives as their political enemies. In Christian Democratic parties in Europe, in contrast, business has to compete for influence with socially-reforming Christian politicians and the Christian trade unions. While it is thus possible to say quite accurately that there is always one party particularly associated with business in contemporary democracies, the extent of business influence within that party, and the type of business which has influence within that party, may vary significantly.

Purpose of Business–Government Relations

It is very easy to assume the universality of what is in fact a particularly Anglo-American perspective on business–government relations. That is to assume that government and business are involved in a necessarily *adversarial* relationship.

  The major political task for business is to limit government policies such as company taxation or regulations which cost business money. In fact, as we have seen even in Britain and the USA, the business–government relationship is more complex. Business wants things from government – such as research funds, commercial representation overseas, and protection from unfair foreign competition. Outside the USA and Britain, the tradition of regarding business and government as necessarily locked in conflict is unfamiliar. In both Germany and Japan industrial development was fostered by government;[17] from the earliest days, the relationship between the two was seen as mutually beneficial. In France, too, there has been a tradition stretching back to Colbert of the duty of government to promote industries. Since the Second World War, business has joined with government (and, to a lesser extent, unions) in the formulation of a Five-year economic Plan. Similarly, the Japanese Ministry of International Trade and Industry (MITI) has developed, and to some degree fostered, a particular view of how Japanese industry should develop, encouraging growth in areas such as computers where the prospects seem bright, and encouraging movement out of industries with limited potential such as textiles, an inherently low-wage industry MITI believed to be fundamentally unsuited to the contemporary Japanese economy.[18]

  Such collaborative links between government and industry have been called 'industrial policy' in Britain and the USA. There is widespread agreement that the USA and Britain are much less likely to have coherent industrial policies than Japan and France. This is partly a matter of ideology. Business executives, politicians (except on the left of the Labour and Democratic Parties) and civil servants are likely to oppose detailed government involvement in industry. Broad-scale management of the economy has long been accepted in

Britain; government policies concerned with the encouragement or discouragement of specific industries have been much less accepted than in France or Japan. Political structures are also relevant here. In both Britain and the USA the political system is very responsive, particularly to geographically-concentrated interests (because in two-party systems a small, strategically placed minority may determine the outcome of a parliamentary or presidential election). In both Japan and France, the power within government of the bureaucracy, the dominance of a single party in Japan, and the weakness of politicians in the French Fourth Republic (followed by the insulation from electoral pressures of the president in the Fifth Republic) have made it easier to make politically unpopular but economically wise decisions.

We can ask, therefore, not only how the character of the business–government relationship varies, but also how its *purposes* vary. Just as countries can be contrasted in terms of the degree to which business–government relations can be described as corporatist, so can countries be contrasted in terms of the degree to which their governments follow a purposeful industrial policy, promoting long-term industrial growth.

'Enemies' of Business

A full consideration of the role of any interest in society should consider not only the characteristics of that interest, but also the attitudes and strength of its potential enemies. As we have stressed above, the character of business organisations can be profoundly affected by the degree to which business executives perceive that common interests of the business community are threatened. However, the success of such organisations in defending business interests will be affected in turn by the organisation, support and resources of any interests with which conflict might develop.

Traditionally, the business community has felt that its common interests are most likely to be threatened by trade unions and socialist movements. There are well-known variations in the degree to which unions constitute a political threat to business. A large section of the American union movement was influenced by a 'business union' conception of their role, represented by the founder of the American Federation of Labor (AFL), Samuel Gompers.

Gompers's belief in pure and simple unionism led him to oppose any broad role for unions in politics, and to argue that union members had an interest in the profitability of their companies; profitable companies could afford larger wage increases than unprofitable companies. Gompers, moreover, believed in the provision of unemployment and sickness insurance through the unions rather than through government. In short, his type of unionism posed few problems for the collective interests of business. In contrast, the industrial unions in the USA, and most European trade unions, have played a much more active political role, typically pressing for welfare state measures unwelcome to business. The variation in the character of unions, both between countries and within the same country over time, means that unions have posed a problem of varying complexity politically for business executives. Moreover, unions obviously differ in strength. Unions have succeeded in recruiting a proportion of the workforce which varies from 20 per cent in the USA and just under 50 per cent in Britain to over 75 per cent in Austria and the Scandinavian countries. Although the percentage of the workforce unionised is not a precise measure of the political power of unions, it is obviously an important influence.

One might argue, however, that in most countries there has been something of an 'historic compromise' between organised labour and organised business. That is in a sense what corporatism is all about. Certainly in Germany there are few contentious issues between the employers' organisation and unions; the Swedish employers' organisation and the union federation, (LO) similarly enjoy smooth relations. Even in Britain, it is probably the case that the Trades Union Congress (TUC) and the CBI agree as much as they disagree, and certainly are on better terms with each other than their American counterparts. Most social democratic parties have similarly made their peace with business in the context of a mixed economy in which there are both publicly- and privately-owned enterprises supporting a welfare state. Only in Britain does the question of the extent of public ownership still seem to arouse the passions. Indeed, it has often seemed that social democratic parties – perhaps because of a belief in planning rather than free markets – have been particularly conspicuous in the creation of highly-institutionalised, corporatist links between business organisations, unions and government. In Britain, the Labour Governments of

1964–70 and 1974–9 were more favourably disposed to close links between government and the CBI than the Conservative Governments which succeeded them. Similarly in the USA, faltering steps towards corporatism under Democratic President Carter (involving exploring the idea of a business, union and government forum) were halted by the election of the vehemently free market Reagan Administration.

Of late, business in several countries has been more concerned about the political consequences of pro-environment, pro-consumer, often middle-class protest than by the activities of the unions. This is not an entirely new phenomenon. Probably the first major political challenge business corporations in the USA faced came not from unions but from middle-class reformers of the Progressive movement. Shocked by the worst excesses of industrialisation, Progressives campaigned for government regulation of the wholesomeness of food and drugs, truth in advertising, and child labour laws. In our own time, American business executives have been distressed by the activities of consumer activists such as Ralph Nader, and environmentalist organisations such as Friends of the Earth. As we shall see, such movements were able to secure a flood of new regulation of business between 1967 and 1974. Business executives have argued that such regulations have imposed significant costs on their enterprises.

The consumer and environmental movements of the USA have been copied with less success in Britain, but in both Japan and Germany have been a real force. Indeed, a new political party in Germany growing out of such movements, the Greens, succeeded in 1983 in passing the 5 per cent of the vote required to win representation in the Bundestag (to prevent fragmentation of the party system, parties winning less than 5 per cent of the vote are denied any seats). Such movements can be a very real source of irritation to business executives. Indeed, right-wing commentators and political scientists in the USA have argued recently that it would be better from their point of view for the USA to have a socialist movement than such implacable reformers.[19]

In the past, farmers were also potential enemies for business. The American populist movement and the communist section of the French peasantry both provided social bases for movements with an anti-capitalist spirit. However, in most countries, even in Germany and Japan, there has been a drift from the land. Agriculture has become larger scale and more like a capitalist enterprise itself. Not surprisingly in view of these developments, the British National Farmers' Union (NFU) is affiliated to the CBI and the largest of the American farmers' organisations (the American Farm Bureau Federation – AFBF) is vehemently pro-business and pro-free market. In short, agrarian protest is no longer a serious problem for business politically. Farmers' organisations may, however, still constitute part of coalitions often ranged against business organisations; the USA NFU is a case in point. Even the British NFU long constituted an important element in the coalition against British membership of the European Economic Community (EEC), a cause much favoured by most business executives at the time. Japanese farmers embarrass the more successful Japanese manufacturing exporters by their ability to extract from the Liberal Party protectionist policies of the kind Japanese industries fear in their export markets.

We may therefore conclude by saying that business executives in different countries and at different times face challenges from different sources. A full treatment of the role of business in any particular country requires consideration of these challenges.

Summary

At one time it might have seemed acceptable to theorise about the relationship between government and business in capitalist societies, as though such relationships were relatively constant. This chapter has stressed the numerous ways in which relations between government, business and politics can vary both within the same country over time, and between different capitalist countries at the same time. The degree to which business is organised politically; the attitudes of the public to business; links between different interests and political parties; the degree to which there are institutionalised ties between business and government; and the degree to which business faces the hostility of organised interests against it all vary from place to place and from time to time. Whereas some theorists (both Marxists and non-Marxists) may have thus wished to emphasise the similarities in the business–government relationship in all capitalist societies, the book which follows is based on the assumption – acceptable to both Marxist and non-Marxist theorists –

that the differences in business–government relations are worth exploring.

The countries chosen for examination in the chapters which follow have been selected precisely to illustrate the variations in business–government relations which exist. We shall examine the countries usually cited as the classic examples of corporatism: Austria and Sweden. Japan, apart from being the world's second largest economy, has been selected because, as is well known, it is the country in which the business community and government have been involved in a particularly close relationship – so close that the label 'Japan Inc.' has been attached to the country. We shall see whether this jibe is justified. France, too, has been celebrated as a country which has successfully blended business and government, not only because the government owns a large number of industries but because the series of Plans drawn up after extensive consultation were seen as underlying the tremendous economic success of France in post-war decades. Great Britain is of equally obvious general interest, though sadly as an example of economic failure rather than success. Britain has alternated between 'corporatist' periods in which government and industry and government and unions have been very closely linked institutionally, and periods when such relations have been deliberately loosened by government. West Germany commands attention as the successful 'social market economy' in which the direct role of government in the economy is veiled and probably limited. Finally, the USA commands attention not only as the world's largest economy but as the country in which capitalism is most politically secure, yet business is the worst organised as a pressure group to protect its collective interests. We shall start with this paradoxical country.

2

Business and Politics in the USA

Support for a Capitalist Market System

Whenever trouble threatens the world, the American dollar strengthens against other currencies. The strength of the dollar reflects the belief amongst investors that the USA is the country in which capitalism is safest. Such interpretations of the strength of business in the USA are common. The comment attributed to Eisenhower's Secretary of Defence that 'what is good for General Motors is good for the United States' may have been a slight misrepresentation of his remarks. The remark was, however, picked up by many as symptomatic of the degree to which capitalism in the USA is unchallenged.

It is indeed the case that most Americans explicitly support a capitalist market system. Opinion polls show that most Americans (69 per cent) are prepared to make sacrifices to defend the free-enterprise system, regard economic freedoms as essential for freedom in general, and are mainly opposed (74 per cent) to any large-scale government ownership of industry.[1] As Shonfield notes,[2] the USA is one of the few countries in which the word 'capitalism' has no opprobrious connotations. In most Western countries – and many Eastern European ones – the practical necessity of using market incentives is widely accepted. In the USA, however, market mechanisms have a degree of moral legitimacy as determinants of the allocation of incomes, resources and investment not commonly found elsewhere. King has argued that government spending in the USA is unusually small by the standards of industrial democracies; government spends a lower proportion of gross national product

(GNP) than in any industrial democracy other than Japan. Nationalised industries are almost unknown; government services such as a national health service or insurance have not been implemented in the USA;[3] and the tendency under President Reagan has been for government to reduce further its commitment to ameliorate poverty. The free-enterprise system is thus unusally free of government 'interference'.

The reasons for the strength of support for capitalism and hostility to extensive powers for government in the USA have been much discussed. Probably the most popular explanations are rooted in an emphasis on the distinctive history of the USA. Louis Hartz,[4] for example, argues that its unique history has caused the USA to remain anchored to the nineteenth-century *liberal traditions* of support for democracy, civil liberties and a market economic system in which government plays a limited role. Having no aristocracy, the USA could not support the paternalistic conservatism of such nineteenth-century Europeans as Shaftesbury, Disraeli or Bismarck. As political rights, including the vote, were extended very speedily to nearly all white men in the USA by 1830 the combination which in Hartz's view was crucial for the development of socialism, a simultaneous quest for economic rights and full citizenship (for example, the right to vote) did not affect the USA. Other writers have stressed different factors in the history of the USA tending in the same direction. American wages have been comparatively high, and the working class has been fragmented by ethnic, racial and regional divisions. The opportunities, real or alleged, for individual advancement through geographic social mobility in addition all protected the legitimacy of capitalism by inhibiting challenges to it.[5] European visitors to the USA in the nineteenth century such as Dickens, de Tocqueville and Sombart noted, too, that the American working class was never as distinct from the middle class in terms of culture, dress or consumption patterns as in Europe. Class consciousness, predictably, was therefore lower. Finally, both the Republican and Democratic Parties established links with the working class at an early stage through the urban machine to a degree untrue of, say, the Liberals in Britain. As in Britain, the electoral system discourages third parties.

Not surprisingly, in view of such factors, the USA is distinctive amongst industrial democracies in that no socialist party has received major support (in 1912, Eugene Debbs received about 7 per cent of the votes cast, or almost one million, which was by far the socialists' best showing in a presidential election). Those identified as socialist or communist have received little support and have suffered persecution in periods such as the years following the Bolshevik *coup* in Russia in 1917, and during the first decade of the Cold War from 1945 to 1955 (an episode somewhat misleadingly named after Senator Joe McCarthy who was by no means the only 'Red baiter'). Of course, such repression, painful as it was, scarcely matched repression in countries such as Russia in which communism triumphed. Unions have also been influenced by such factors. The oldest unions in the USA are by and large craft unions[6] which struggled to find respectability by confining themselves to a narrow, instrumentalist approach to politics. These craft unions formed the American Federation of Labor (AFL). Union involvement in politics was confined to issues affecting their rights, or which strengthened their bargaining position, such as the exclusion of Chinese labourers.

A very different type of union gained ground in the 1930s, typically industry-wide, based on mass production or heavy industries such as steel or cars. These unions, which formed the Congress of Industrial Organizations (CIO), shared a generally social democratic approach to politics, the most famous exemplar being Walter Reuther of the United Auto Workers who became President of the CIO. But though the AFL's differences with the CIO became sufficiently less intense for the organisations to merge in 1955, the 'business union' approach which the craft unions had embodied remained important both within the AFL–CIO and within certain unions expelled from it, notably the Teamsters. Union membership in the USA has moreover lagged below the levels common in northern Europe. Union membership in the USA peaked at 35 per cent shortly after the Second World War, and has since fallen to around 20 per cent of the workforce. There are large parts of the USA (such as the South and South-West), in which the unions are conspicuously weak. As these areas (and industries nation-wide in which unions are traditionally weak, such as services) are the fastest-growing in the USA, the unions look certain to continue to decline.

A Bed of Roses for Business?

It may seem, on the basis of the facts we have covered so far, that the American business executive has no political problems. Such, in reality, would not be the case. Although the basic features of capitalism are not contested in the USA, there has been at least as much (and possibly more) criticism of the day-to-day conduct of corporations in the USA than in any other industrial democracy. Opinion polls show, for example, that most Americans are in favour of strict regulation of such undesirable by-products of industry as pollution, workplace accidents or occupationally caused illness and unsafe consumer goods.[7]

In the late 1960s and early 1970s, such sentiments found expression in newly-created or rejuvenated public-interest groups. Capitalising on the growth in a middle-class propensity to participate in politics, increased cynicism amongst Americans over business, government and other major institutions, organisations such as Friends of the Earth, the Sierra Club and Common Cause succeeded in imposing constraints on corporations in such diverse aspects of their activities as discharges into rivers or lakes and discharges of funds to politicians as bribes or campaign contributions. Though the influence of public-interest groups declined in the late 1970s for a variety of reasons (including increased fears of inflation and the uncompetitiveness of American industry with consequent loss of jobs) the public-interest groups had secured the adoption of important laws constraining many aspects of business behaviour.

Such a 'surge and decline' in criticism of business producing some permanent results is by no means an unusual phenomenon in the USA. The 'revolt' of poor farmers demanding government controls over banks and railroads contributed to the adoption of legislation affecting those industries, even though within twenty years the Populist movement was dead. The Progressives, a loose alliance of reforming intellectuals, writers and journalists, were equally ephemeral but contributed to an even greater amount of reforming legislation on monopoly, clean food and drugs, and other constraints on business abuses. Franklin Roosevelt's New Deal alliance of the South, farmers, unions, ethnic groups, northern cities and intellectuals lasted in its full glory for only eight years, yet changed fundamentally (and permanently) the balance between business and government power in the USA. Such challenges to business may be temporary, but are nonetheless important in their consequences.

Neither is it the case that government officials in the USA are necessarily sympathetic or close to business. Although it is true that there have been periods in which officials of agencies such as the

Interstate Commerce Commission (ICC) were seen as being too favourably disposed to the industry which they supposedly regulated in the interests of the public, there have been other periods (such as the 1970s) when the officials of agencies such as the Federal Trade Commission (FTC), the Environmental Protection Agency (EPA) and Occupational Safety and Health Administration (OSHA) were bitterly attacked by businessmen as being either uncomprehending of their problems, or even actively hostile to business. Some academic writers concluded that American government was actually more stringent in its regulation of business than the governments of supposedly more left-wing countries.[8] Moreover, the strength of the *laissez-faire* tradition in the USA denied government an active role in partnership with industry in an 'industrial policy', as developed in France and Japan (except when, as in the case of defence industries, a special factor such as national security legitimated government intervention).

It is also misleading to think of the USA as a country in which government exists on a nineteenth-century scale. The growth in government in the USA may have been slower than elsewhere, but the share of GNP spent by governments (federal, state and local) is now one-third. Government, in short, is a major potential customer, and one whose purchases are often affected by political pressures. Moreover, as Shonfield noted, although there are practically no nationalised industries in the USA, regulation has generally been more extensive and stringent than in other countries. Anti-monopoly legislation was tougher than in Britain, water polluters prosecuted more vigorously than in Britain, and health and safety at work legislation imposed more toughly than in much more socialist Sweden. The importance of government as a customer and the problems which could arise with potential regulators meant that there were plenty of political issues for business to worry about. The celebrated popularity of capitalism as an abstract doctrine has not produced a problem-free life for capitalists.

Defending Business Interests: A Multi-Pronged Approach

The modern American corporation is likely to follow a variety of approaches in defending its interests. The approach used will depend partly on the nature of the issue, but will also often involve several complementary strategies which can be used simultaneously.

The wise corporation will try to create a favourable *attitude* and willingness to listen amongst decision-makers before a problem arises. The most obvious way to do this is through campaign contributions. Prior to 1972 it was common for corporations to make campaign contributions from their general funds. This practice was illegal, and so such contributions were often routed through overseas subsidiaries or individual donations by corporate executives in order to disguise their origin. After the Watergate affair led to the discovery of such illegal campaign contributions, corporations were limited to contributing amounts of no more than $5000 per candidate per election, the money to be raised by political action committees (PACs). Though PACs can have their operating expenses paid by the corporation, their funds must be 'voluntary' contributions from executives or stockholders. A corporation's PAC may also ask its workers to contribute on two occasions a year – a rarely-used procedure.

Company PACs generally concentrate their giving on those best placed to help the company. Corporations thus usually give most of their money to incumbents (politicians already in Congress) rather than to their challengers. Such beneficiaries will usually be on the Congressional committees that most affect the corporation. Corporations' PACs have proved willing to contribute to Democrats, even liberal Democrats who are in the powerful positions and are almost certain to be re-elected, because the object is to buy access to the legislator and, if possible, goodwill. Only in 1978 when the political tide was running against the Democrats did corporation PACs follow their hearts and tilt heavily towards supporting Republicans.

The corporation would also expect support from *Representatives* and *Senators* from areas where its factories are located. Such assistance might be of particular importance when there is competition between corporations for a government contract, for example to build a new transport plane for the Air Force. The top executives of the company can attempt to build ties to the legislators by making individual contributions to their campaign funds, though since 1974 such contributions have been limited by law to $1000 per election. The executives may also participate directly in the campaign, though this is unlikely. In spite of being urged frequently to become more involved politically, company executives have usually been too busy to do so. Social contacts and links with other local élites (through working for the local symphony orchestra, for example) may however provide an opportunity for influencing the local climate of opinion and so, indirectly, the legislator. Above all, however, the legislator is likely to feel an identity of interest with local companies. Local companies, after all, determine the income and employment prospects of the legislator's voters. The American system provides numerous opportunities for the legislator to claim the credit for good news for local companies: defence contracts, for example, will generally be announced through the local legislator's office.

A third line of attack which the corporation might use would be to exploit links with the *Executive branch*. These links will take a variety of forms. The most obvious links are personal. Both Democratic and Republican Administrations recruit heavily from the ranks of business executives to fill the thousands of political appointments made by the president. Key figures of the first Reagan Administration (1980–4), such as George Schultz, the Secretary of State, came to Washington from the boardrooms of major corporations (in Schultz's case, the Bechtel Corporation). These personal links can be used if the corporation has a problem which needs government action or assistance. The awareness of the value that personal connections can provide in American corporations is demonstrated by the lucrative careers that former Executive branch officials can have as a company lobbyists; a similarly lucrative career also awaits defeated legislators, whose Congressional contacts are greatly prized.

Apart from such personal ties, corporations may have almost institutionalised ties to particular government *agencies*. The agencies are subjected to constant argument and pleading from companies whose business is affected by their work. Corporations can moreover make life unpleasant for agencies that cross them through their Congressional allies. Congressional committee assignments are typically given to legislators with a constituency interest in the committee's work. The committees that supply agencies with operating funds or that oversee their work are thus typically filled with legislators representing the people (including corporations, their executives and workers) with which agencies have to deal. The agency which offends interests it supposedly controls risks having its budget savaged and its executives humiliated by representatives of those interests in Congress.

Such considerations have led many observers to argue that American government agencies are unusually susceptible to 'capture' by the interests with which they deal. Agencies can be coerced as well as persuaded to fall in with their 'clients" view of good public policy. Yet such arguments can be taken too far by neglecting the importance of party politics. Democratic Administrations have been quite likely to appoint people more sympathetic to environmental protection or labour unions to key positions, while the Republicans have appointed quite consistently officials sympathetic to business. In spite of predictions of capture by business, Democratic appointees to agencies such as the National Labor Relations Board (NLRB), the EPA, the OSHA and the FTC have caused apoplexy in the boardrooms of corporate America. Individual companies are usually represented in Washington by law firms. These are not law firms which specialise in court appearances, indeed, many of the law firms' senior partners have not set foot in a court for decades. 'Lawyers' such as the one-time Truman presidential aide Clark Clifford, sell not their legal expertise but their connections, connections built up over the years with a wide variety of influential people in Congress and the Executive branch. Access to such power figures might not secure a favourable decision for the company, but it will at least secure a serious hearing for the company's arguments.

Individual companies in the USA thus have numerous opportunities to influence decisions before they need the assistance of a trade association or an 'umbrella organisation' for employers. Somewhat surprisingly, American trade associations and employers' organisations have not enjoyed a consistently high reputation in recent decades.

Modes of Political Participation

Writers in the late 1950s and early 1960s were struck by the limited development of business organisations in the USA. The groups claiming to speak for the general interests of business were notoriously weak. Both the Chamber of Commerce and the National Association of Manufacturers (NAM) were regarded as highly ideological assocations with little to contribute to the discussion of complex policy issues. One authority found substance in the rumour that the NAM was the 'kiss of death' for a cause which it supported.[9] Neither did trade associations seem stronger. In their magisterial study of the impact of business on American trade policy, Bauer, Pool and Dexter[10] found that trade associations were accorded little prestige. Business executives regarded the staff of the associations as people incapable of 'making it' in business, while the lobbyists of trade associations were by and large dependent on the goodwill of politicians already disposed to support them. Politicians were more likely to complain about the paucity of information provided by both trade assocations, or about the failure of trade associations even to contact undecided Representatives and Senators than to complain about pressure from them. Trade associations were neither a major source of information nor regarded as the authoritative voice of business. The picture of trade associations painted by Bauer, Pool and Dexter is more of organisations anxiously trying to maintain membership than of organisations exerting pressure successfully on politicians.

The weakness of trade associations and 'umbrella groups' representing the general interest of business contrasted with the growth of such organisations in Europe and Japan. The USA lacked interest-group representatives who were recognised by the government, Congress, the media and the public as the authoritative voice of business. Instead, the business organisations of the USA seemed weak, ideological and bitterly divided.

This organisational weakness represented, ironically, political strength.[11] Business organised little to protect its collective interests in the USA in the 1950s because its collective interests were little challenged. A variety of factors contributed to the political strength of business. Opinion polls showed a high degree of public confidence in business executives and major companies. The Eisenhower Administration not only pursued pro-business policies, but at the highest levels was overwhelmingly recruited from the ranks of business executives. In Congress, a pro-business conservative coalition of Republicans and southern Democrats controlled the agenda, and its southern Democrat members benefited from the workings of the 'seniority system' under which the most senior members of the majority parties received the tremendously powerful chairmanships of Congressional committees. Moreover, though their legality was sometimes questionable, contributions to the campaigns of both Republicans and Democrats of business executives or stockholders were the most important source of election campaign funds for both parties. A general assault on business was not, therefore, to be feared.

A number of factors in the late 1960s and 1970s convinced American business executives that more vigorous action was needed to protect their collective interests. There was a very sharp decline in confidence in business and business executives amongst the public, exceeding the rate of decline of trust in other American institutions. The balance of power in Congress changed in a way which favoured conservatives less and liberals more, while public-interest groups seeking legislation protecting the environment and public from harmful side-effects of business activity scored notable triumphs, reflecting a considerable upsurge in their membership, funding and prestige. The Watergate affair brought disgrace to not only President Nixon but also to those business executives who had made illegal contributions to his election campaign, generally under pressure from the Administration and fearful of government harrassment if they did not comply. New campaign finance laws both reduced the possibilities for illegal campaign contributions by business executives and created new opportunities for pressure groups to raise funds for election campaigns through the PACS.

The factor which above all else caused alarm in business circles was the increased impact of government regulation. One of the largest-ever increases in government regulation occurred between 1967 and 1976. This entailed not only a five-fold increase in the number of staff employed in the regulatory agencies and a similar increase in their budgets, but also a dramatic increase in the impact of regulation on business. Regulatory agencies had been a feature of American government since the late nineteenth century. Most of the older regulatory agencies had been concerned with the prices and conditions of service of a single industry. The regulatory agencies created in the 1960s and 1970s were generally concerned with the regulation of factors such as pollution and safety which cut across industries, and were often referred to as the social regulatory agencies.

The social regulatory agencies such as the OSHA or the EPA brought the power of federal government to bear on the day-to-day operations of businesses for the first time. Until their creation inspectors encountered by business executives had, by and large, been officials of state governments. The officials of the federal social regulatory agencies were made of sterner stuff than most state officials. The new social regulatory agencies gained a reputation for toughness, and even for adopting an adversarial approach to business. Moreover, the regulations evolved by the social regulatory agencies to protect the environment were extremely costly to business, forcing executives to divert a substantial proportion of investment funds to meeting their requirements.

In brief, the growth of regulation in the 1960s and 1970s seemed to business executives to constitute a dramatic and threatening extension of the power of government. Both the cost and extent of regulation seemed likely to increase, moreover, as time passed. New regulatory agencies, and new regulations from them, seemed all too likely to be created because the liberal Democratic triumphs in the elections following the downfall of President Nixon seemed to suggest the future dominance of politicians critical of business. American business executives, for the first time since the New Deal, feared that government posed a threat to interests shared by a wide variety of business, or what might be termed business's common interests.

The political response of business in the USA to these threats has been vigorous and has occurred at the firm, industry and national levels. Individual firms have increased the number of executives committed to lobbying. Firms have also taken full advantage of the provisions of the 1974 Federal Elections Finance Act, which allowed unions and companies to pay the expenses of the PACs which we have discussed above. In the case of companies, PACs could raise money from shareholders, senior management and, on two occasions a year, from company employees. PACs are operated not only by individual firms but also by trade associations. Together business PACs have rapidly emerged as the most important type of PAC, raising more than twice as much as union PACs, the next most important category.

Dramatic changes have also occurred at levels beyond the individual firm. Most trade associations have been transformed into effective and prestigious organisations. In place of the ineffective organisations described by Bauer, Pool and Dexter have come much more technically proficient trade associations, with higher subscriptions, higher budgets and more technical expertise. Change has been greatest in trade associations for industries such as the chemical manufacturing industry which have felt particularly threatened by the increase in regulation. Trade associations have also tended to move their headquarters to Washington, reflecting the increased importance they attach to political work (rather than to general image creation or technical matters).

Perhaps the most striking change of all has been in the general business organisations. As mentioned earlier, in the 1950s the Chamber of Commerce and the NAM were thought of as negative,` highly ideological organisations finding little favour or prestige outside the far right wing of American politics. Partly because of the low prestige of these organisations, large corporations decided to create a new organisation – the Business Roundtable – to defend their interests. The Business Roundtable was to have a very different style, stressing the technocratic competence of its officials rather than the conservative dogma stressed by the Chamber of Commerce and the NAM. Partly because of this technocratic image, the Business Roundtable quickly established enormous prestige. President Carter treated the Chairman of the Business Roundtable, Irving Shapiro of Dupont, as *the* voice of big business, and many Representatives and Senators followed his lead.

The older business umbrella organisations did not allow the challenge from the Business Roundtable to go unanswered. The NAM and Chamber of Commerce made a futile attempt at merger; thereafter both sought to improve their efficiency and to shed their highly conservative image. The Chamber of Commerce developed a reputation as one of the most effective and vigorous lobbyists in Washington, pioneering techniques in 'grass-roots lobbying' so that the local Chambers of Commerce would be stirred into action, putting pressure on Representatives and Senators in time to change their votes on crucial legislation. In brief, the Chamber of Commerce passed from being one of the most derided to one of the most admired of the American pressure groups. The Chamber of Commerce reached a high point of prestige with the advent of the Reagan Administration, even giving it lists of civil servants it wanted to be dismissed for being unsympathetic to business.

This change illustrated a general change in the standing of business groups in the USA. Whereas once business pressure group officials had sat at the feet of officials from public-interest groups such as Common Cause to learn how to improve their political performance, now the business groups were regarded as the pacesetters. In consequence, even before the elections of 1978 and 1980 brought major gains for conservatives, the improved business lobby had demonstrated a capacity to defeat the unions on proposals to change the labour relations laws in their favour and to stem the advance of the public-interest groups whose proposals for the creation of a consumer advocacy agency were surprisingly defeated in Congress.

Finally, business tried to reverse the tendency for liberal critics of business to dominate American intellectual life. The pro-business American Enterprise Institute (AEI) was the most conspicuous beneficiary of an increased willingness of American executives to wage the war of ideas by funding 'think tanks' likely to support their interest.

Impact of the Reagan Administration and Importance of the Republican Party

The Republican Party has been the more reliable party from business's point of view. E. E. Schattschneider remarked that the Republican Party was business's greatest political resource.[12] Although, because of the ill-disciplined, incoherent nature of American political parties, the Democrats have an important conservative, pro-business wing based primarily in the South and have been dependent on the rich for campaign contributions,[13] the Republican Party in Congress has been overwhelmingly pro-business on issues such as the rights of management *v.* the rights of unions. Yet the Republican Party is not monolithic either, and important divisions affecting business have been apparent. A moderate wing (based in the North-East and associated with large, established companies and Wall Street financial institutions) dominated the party from 1936 until 1964. Its presidential candidates accepted reforms brought in by Democratic Administrations and nominated presidential candidates such as Eisenhower who could plausibly occupy the 'middle ground' of American politics. A more vigorously conservative wing of the party, in contrast, sought to 'roll back' the advance of 'big government' by reducing government expenditures on welfare, the rights of unions and government 'interference' with business through regulation. This right wing of the Republican Party enjoyed the support of small 'Main Street' business, and from the growing industries of the South and South-West. Its presidential candidates – Taft, Goldwater, and Reagan – were committed to a more radical contraction of government than other Republicans thought politically possible (or practically desirable).

The advent of the Reagan Administration brought to power an administration widely supported by business executives. The business community had, in fact, diverse reasons for supporting the Reagan Administration. One group, which had been more favourable towards George Bush than to Reagan in the primary elections to select the Republican candidate, had comparatively modest hopes for a reduction in taxation and in the 'burden' of regulation, and a more balanced federal budget. A more radical group hoped for an even sharper reduction in taxation than in government expenditure, which they still wished to see reduced. Their prediction, supported by Reagan but labelled 'voodoo economics' by Bush, was that a sharp reduction in taxation would stimulate the economy so much on the 'supply side' through improving incentives that any loss of revenue to the government would soon be made up.

The Reagan Administration in office fully satisfied neither camp, but came closest to giving the moderates what they sought. Cuts in taxation, for companies and highly-paid individuals pleased business executives, as did the activities of a Task Force on Regulatory Relief headed by Vice-President George Bush (candidate Bush's references to Reagan's 'voodoo economics' were conveniently forgotten). The reduction in taxation was not deep enough to count as supply-side economics, though the political and practical difficulties in reducing domestic expenditure while decreasing taxation and increasing defence expenditure produced a massive budget deficit, which in turn helped raise interest rates to uncomfortable levels. Discontent with the budget deficit and high interest rates was, however, mitigated by the awareness of business executives that the administration, which contained many people drawn from their ranks, favoured management's interests on issue after issue. The cancelling (or non-enforcement) of safety or environmental regulations opposed by the business community, the opening up of federally-controlled land to mineral developers, and the hostility of the administration to most unions marked sharp reversals of the previous administration's policies. The election of the most right-wing, ideological President since the New Deal did more to change policy in business's favour than all the improvements in business's interest group techniques put together. Party politics, in short, matter as much as interest-group politics.

Industrial Policy

A number of writers have argued that the relationship between business and government is not too close, but in fact too distant. American growth rates have lagged behind the growth rates of more corporatist nations in which business–government relations are more closely organised. At the top and bottom points in the economic cycle American inflation and unemployment rates have been worse than in the more corporatist countries. Such points have strengthened calls in the USA for an industrial policy through which American government would provide assistance for new or ailing industries, probably in return for promises from management and unions for improvements in investment, productivity and performance.

Advocates of industrial policy in the USA have noticed an important fact. For all the election campaign contributions, lobbying and recruitment of business executives into both Republican and Democratic Administrations, the organised links between business and government in the USA are weak. Even now, no single body enjoys the prestige of the CBI in Britain, let alone the Keidanren in Japan. The role of business is seen as a very *political* role, exerting pressure on government, as it were, from the outside rather than being linked into a working relationship *with* government. American industries – with the exception of defence industries – do not benefit from the assistance of government agencies whose job it is to foster their development in the way that MITI in Japan has fostered the development of industries there.

It is more debatable whether this situation could be changed.[14] The USA lacks both the centralised, disciplined form of government and the monopolistic, centralised interest groups of the more corporatist countries. Apart from the division of government into the often conflicting branches of judiciary, Congress and Executive, the Executive branch itself probably suffers from more fragmentation than most systems of government. The departments and agencies are likely to pursue their own policies without much co-ordination, unless the President has unusually clear policies and can find political appointees who share his views to implement them. Members of Congressional committees are often linked to a particular interest (for example, Democrats on the House Education and Labor Committee are allied to unions), so that interest can often control legislation which affects it. The individual Representative or Senator is expected to use his or her considerable power to secure favourable treatment for the district or state. In short, the selective strategy required by an industrial policy – picking some industries to foster and regarding others as industries to be allowed to die – is one which it is extremely difficult to reconcile with the fragmented, particularistic nature of American government.

It is notable in this context that in the fairly numerous cases where government and industry have become closely intertwined, the public interest has clearly suffered. Industries have been more likely to take over or dominate government than government to direct industries in a manner conducive to the national interest. The oil industry thus used American government to boost its profits through tax concessions such as the oil depletion allowance without being required to undertake any action to alleviate America's long-term energy problems. The textile industry secured generous tariff and non-tariff protection against foreign competition without being required to evolve any long-term strategy. The defence industries, though dependent on government for contracts, finance and technical advice, have been able to secure overly generous profits, and possibly to induce excessive levels of defence expenditure or duplicative or unnecessary schemes. If good industrial policy required government to be able to take a steady, coherent view of industrial policy and to direct it in line with the public interest, the risk would be considerable that in the USA industrial policy would be more of a licence to interest groups to advance their goals than a partnership in which either balance or government dominance was maintained.

Nevertheless, it can be argued that all governments have an industrial policy, even if it is by default when they do not realise the implications of their actions. The USA may thus well actually have policies which together constitute a 'policy towards industry', without realising it. The combined effect of such policies towards industries is obviously difficult and contentious to analyse. Government assistance to the defence industries both diverts resources (including skilled manpower) from more productive resources and fosters the development of new products, metals and technologies.

It is almost certainly the case that regulatory agenices in the USA in the 1970s adopted a more adversarial approach towards industry than their counterparts in countries such as Sweden or Great Britain. Such an adversarial approach may have imposed onerous cost burdens on industries; it may also have increased the pressures on industries to modernise (the textile industry, for example, was forced to modernise by the stringent cotton dust regulations imposed on it by the OSHA). The piecemeal character of policies towards industries in the USA makes it particularly difficult to evaluate their effect.

Regulation

Government in the USA has less impact on industry than in most industrialised countries in that there is almost no nationalised industry, and government spends a lower proportion of GNP. Regulation – the issuing of orders affecting business by specialist agencies entrusted by Congress with the power to make and enforce orders – is, however, more common. Practically all the industries in the USA which Europeans would expect to find in government ownership are subject instead to government regulation. As we have seen, the growth of social regulation was in itself a powerful influence on business executives, prompting an increase in their political activities.

The nature of the regulatory relationship between government and business in the USA has prompted much contradictory theorising. The older theories on regulation were concerned to explain the failure of regulation due to the 'capture' or domination of regulatory agencies by the industry they supposedly controlled. A variety of reasons were advanced to explain the demise of the regulatory agencies. Some stressed the practical and administrative difficulties of operating without the goodwill of the regulated. Regulations are harder to devise if industry is unwilling to share information with the regulators; regulations cannot be enforced effectively unless most firms co-operate voluntarily, for the number of inspectors is never adequate to cover every workplace. Other writers stressed the temptation held out to officials of better-paid jobs in industry in the future in return for their sympathetic treatment of the industry in the present – a system known as the 'revolving door'. Yet others stressed the importance of the fact that regulatory agencies, given independence of the president and Congress by law, could rely on neither for support in conflicts with business. Bernstein summarised these discontents in what is perhaps the single most influential book on the subjects.[15] Bernstein argued that regulatory agencies passed through a life cycle of vigorous youth, conciliatory middle age and senility. In youth, the regulatory agency, supported by a political movement which had secured its creation, fought many battles with its industry. In middle age, the decline of the political movement which had created it, and the mounting practical, administrative and legal difficulties of fighting the industry it confronted, induced a more conciliatory attitude in the agency. In old age, the agency succumbed to the steady pressures from its industry, not matched by any pressures on behalf of the public, and adopted pro-industry attitudes.

Ironically, most of the recent writing on regulation in the USA has been concerned with the problem of 'regulatory unreasonableness'.[16] Regulators in the USA were likely, it was argued, to impose ridiculously costly requirements on industry in return for negligible benefits. Regulators in the USA were also likely to impose these regulations in a harsher, less sensible mannner than regulators in countries such as Sweden or Britain. The unreasonableness of regulators in the USA was a function of both culture and law. The culture of the USA is adversarial; individuals assert their rights against each other vigorously, frequently resorting to law to resolve differences, and being less likely to compromise differences (especially with government) than peoples of other countries. Moreover, the emphasis in American law on equal treatment for all inhibits the exercise of sensible discretion by regulatory agencies. Instead, officials of regulatory agencies are more likely to 'go by the book', applying regulations in an arid, uncompromising manner.

The diametrically opposed nature of these two arguments probably reflects the weakness of both. Too much theorising about regulation in the USA overlooks the importance of politics. The theories of regulatory failure referred to a period when there were few powerful critics of business in the USA. The theories of regulatory unreasonableness refer to the period in which the critics of business, particularly in the public-interest groups, were at their strongest. The nature of regulatory legislation, the pressures exerted through the presidency, courts and Congress, differed accordingly.

It is important to note in this context how the election of President Reagan emasculated the regulatory agencies which had incurred the wrath of business. The OSHA and EPA reversed policy completely, passing from being regarded as anti- to pro-business in a matter of months, discarding in the process former friends in the unions and environmental protection groups.

The change also reminds us that the nature of regulation can vary tremendously. Calls for 'deregulation' came both from the left and right in American politics. Yet the question 'Who benefits?' draws different answers from agency to agency. The Civil Aeronautics Board (CAB) helped airlines maintain high fares and profits at the expense of the public. The EPA, prior to the election of President Reagan, exerted a substantial downward pressure on business profits because of the vigour with which it pursued environmental protection. Like many aspects of government, regulation is a weapon which can be used to the advantage or disadvantage of different interests. The impact of regulation, therefore, is determined by political conflicts, not by the nature of the process itself.

State and Local Government

Our focus so far has been on the federal level of government. Yet the thousands of state and local governments of the USA are also of great potential importance to business. The adoption by California, for example, of its own pollution control law governing car exhaust fumes complicates life considerably for car companies. The adoption of laws banning the use of non-returnable drink containers by a number of states causes similar complications for brewers and soft drink manufacturers.

It is a tribute to the perverted priorities of political science that so much more has been written on the power of business at the local level (in the so-called 'community power' debate[17]) in the USA than at the national level. Apart from the fact that any power élite which business might dominate in the USA might not care who ran towns such as New Haven, the local communities and states of the USA differ sufficiently to make generalisation hazardous. Even contiguous states such as Wisconsin and Illinois have radically different approaches to business and politics, the former being much less tolerant than the latter of anything constituting corruption. It is not surprising, either, given differences in political culture, political participation and economic circumstances that whereas some studies have found no evidence of significant business power in the city studied, others have found the opposite.

It is often suggested that in general the power of business is likely to be greater at the state and local than at the national level. A variety of factors are advanced in support of this claim. Participation rates in state are lower than in federal politics, so that the power of interest groups may be higher than in federal politics. The prevalence of corruption in state and local politics has generally been thought higher than in federal politics, and business interests are generally better placed than most to benefit financially. Above all, state and local governments can be intimidated more easily by business threats to locate elsewhere if treated in a manner that business deems unsatisfactory.

The practical significance of threats to locate elsewhere is difficult to assess, partly because it is easier for firms in some industries than others to move. Whereas the textile industry, partly attracted by low wages, weak unions and sympathetic governments, has indeed moved from the North-East to the South of the USA, the opportunities for coal or uranium mining firms to move are severely restricted in the short and medium terms (in the long term, exploration may be focused outside areas with 'unsympathetic business climates'). Business magazines regularly evaluate the business climate in different states, but the nature of these evaluations is more complex than might be supposed. The level of company taxation, for example, which one might think to be of obvious importance to business executives, was regarded by them in the 1983 survey as only the thirteenth most important factor in deciding where to locate.[18] Though a cheap, docile workforce may be of paramount importance to the textile industry, factors requiring high levels of government expenditure – such as an educated workforce, cultural facilities for top executives and good schools for their children – may weigh more heavily with, say, the microchip companies. It is no accident that the conservative policies of the Southern states have brought them few technologically advanced industries.

Though there are grounds for scepticism, therefore, about the likelihood of businesses relocating because of the policies of state and local governments, there are fewer grounds for doubting what effect the fear of such moves has on the policies of such governments. Indeed, in recent years states have experienced a worrying fall in their revenues because of competition between them to attract businesses through tax cuts and exemptions for industries investing within their jurisdiction. The recession of the early 1980s and its associated high levels of unemployment raised to fever pitch worries amongst state officials about the 'business climate' of their states, thus providing employers' groups at the state and local level with a great opportunity to change policies they disliked.

Conclusions

The popularity of the dollar on the foreign exchanges during periods of crisis reflects the accurate perception that the future of capitalism in the USA is more secure than in almost any other country. There is no socialist movement of any significance in the USA, and unions are unusually weak. But there are at least temporary problems for business to handle. Public-interest groups have been stronger and more successful than in most countries in securing limitations on business through regulation. Moreover, the relationship between business and government is less structured and less formally integrated than in more corporatist countries. The trade associations and 'umbrella' groups speaking for business in the USA are generally accorded less respect and access to decision-makers than their counterparts in other countries. Moreover, the USA does not have, and is not likely to have, the sort of comprehensive industrial policies designed to foster growth which countries such as France and Japan regard as normal.

What are the prospects for change? In the 1970s the mounting challenge to business from public-interest groups at home and foreign competition abroad seemed likely to change business–government relations considerably. The strengthened business organisations, in particular the Business Roundtable, seemed likely to develop formalised relations with government reminiscent of employers' organisations in other countries. The advent of the pro-business Reagan Administration has, however, reduced the impetus for change. Business is more active politically than it used to be, and is more successful in its activities. In contrast, the political opponents of business in unions or the public-interest groups have been forced on to the defensive by declining membership, a public opinion now more concerned about prices and American competitiveness than about social goals, and an Administration committed to a pro-business approach. The pressures on American business to change fundamentally its approach to politics have diminished. American business, therefore, by international standards, looks vigorously and effectively involved in politics, though in a relatively disorganised manner. The absense of an umbrella group which can claim to be *the* voice of business, the openness of the links between the Chamber of Commerce or the NAM and the right wing of American politics, and the limited consultation of trade associations by government agencies when formulating policy continue to surprise the foreigner. Yet the foreign exchanges in crises demonstrate by the popularity of the dollar international confidence in the future of capitalism in the USA, showing again that the political and organisational strength of business are significantly different issues.

3

Business and Politics in West Germany

The Social Market Economy

In the last twenty years the economies which have been hailed as economic miracles are newly-industrialised nations such as South Korea, Taiwan, Singapore, Brazil and (though with a longer history of industrialisation) Japan. It is easy to forget, therefore, that the term 'economic miracle' was first applied to West Germany. From the ruins of 1945, West Germany has surged forward economically, not only surpassing the British economy but equalling (in terms of real living standards) the USA. In the thirty years after the Second World War, West Germany became established as the industrial powerhouse of Western Europe, the industrial locomotive to which other European countries would look for the economic power to drag them out of recession. The growth of the German economy was a phenomenal achievement by a people so reduced in circumstances in 1945 that the average daily calorie intake (at 1451) was less than half the figure for 1936 (3113).[1]

Many factors contributed to the miracle. The German capacity for hard work, high-quality work and discipline was a great advantage. The influx of refugees from eastern Europe after the war (and from East Germany until the building of the Berlin Wall) brought social problems such as an exacerbated housing shortage, but also provided West Germany with a skilled workforce which, like most immigrants, was willing to work exceptionally hard. The surplus of labour created first by these immigrants and then by the very large-scale influx of 'guest workers' from countries such as Turkey and Yugoslavia helped restrain the rate of increase of wages and the power of unions. The war had not destroyed German industry to anything like the extent popularly imagined; Allied bombing was so insufficiently focused on industrial targets that German industrial capacity was greater at the end of the war than the start.[2]

The German economy was well positioned, therefore, to profit from the demand unleashed by Western rearmament, the Korean War and the general economic boom of the 1950s. Undoubtedly the West Germans did benefit – probably more than anyone else – from capital supplied by the USA under the Marshall Plan for post-war European recovery. The end of the Nazi era also provided an opportunity for wiping the slate clean socially, if not always industrially. The British occupying authorities, implementing a policy which their own unions would not have accepted, were instrumental in ensuring that the reconstituted trades unions, which had been proscribed by the Nazis, were organised on a rational basis (usually industry-wide) and were comparatively few in number. The size and industry-wide character of the new German unions enabled them to take a longer view of their members' interests while British unions were locked in demarcation disputes.

Though West Germany faced very severe problems in the aftermath of the Second World War, the country did, of course, have an industrial structure which was long established. In that sense, West Germany was in a very different position to the newly-industrialised countries or even France. The problem in West Germany was reviving industries and markets, not creating them from scratch. It is debatable, therefore, whether there was ever in West Germany quite the same opportunity for government to take the leading role that there was in France or Japan where opportunities had to be discovered and developed from scratch. In any event, government in West Germany was not inclined to play such a leading role. On the contrary, indicative planning of the French type or the government–industry partnership of the Japanese type were consciously rejected. Instead, the West Germans officially adopted as a guide to their policies the doctrine of the 'social market economy'. The social market economy was a doctrine at first articulated by academics from the University of Freiburg but popularised, and to some degree implemented, by Ludwig Erhard, first as Economic Adviser for the Western Zone, then as federal Minister of Finance under Adenauer, and finally as federal Chancellor himself.[3]

At first sight, the principles of the social market economy look identical to the principles of *laissez-faire* economics. Government should not intervene in individual industries, nor should they accept responsibility for macro-economic management. The principles of monetarism were popular in West Germany long before they were in Britain and the USA, and Keynes was conversely less popular. The aim of government, apart from providing the general infrastructure for the economy, should be to foster competition, both through attacking monopolies and cartels and through fostering freer international trade. It is important to emphasise that in the German context these were quite novel doctrines. As many writers have noted, German industrialisation, in contrast to British and American experience, was the result of co-operation between highly concentrated industry and the state. In an alliance between the Prussian states, eager for the military might that the industrialisation of Germany would bring, and the industrialists such as Krupp who created the industrial empires, rapid industrialisation took place behind high tariff barriers fostered by government finance. This pattern of close government–industry co-operation continued throughout the Nazi era, although the balance of power between the industrialists and Hitler remains a matter of great historical controversy. The economic principles of the social market economy resonate with the liberal traditions of Britain and the USA. The principles involved a sharp break not only with the protectionism, planning, cartelisation and subjection of economic to nationalist aspirations which had characterised the Nazi era but also with the general pattern of business–government relations in German history.

What, it might be asked, was distinctively 'social' about a social market economy which stressed competition and keeping government at arm's length from the day-to-day operations of industry? The advocates of the social market economy did argue that they saw a major role for government. Government was to use its power to promote the social market economy by attacking monopoly cartels, etc. Government was also to take action to correct the failings of the market economy, to provide such social services as were necessary to correct poverty, maldistribution of incomes and pollution – evils which would not be corrected through market mechanisms. In a sense, the 'social' part of the social market economy may be the part which was the more fulfilled. The West

German welfare state is much more generous than the British variant, let alone the fragmented and incomplete American welfare state.

It is less certain that the social market economy ever displaced the more traditional structure that was rooted in German economic history. Culture, tradition, the political power of business and the desire of the Western allies (particularly the Americans) for rapid recovery tended to subvert the social market economy's stress on competition. Within ten years of Germany's defeat, the very same cartels and giant firms which had been blamed in part for the rise of Hitler were again established. Strong efforts had been made to fragment and localise the banking system, but a series of mergers in the 1950s and 1960s re-established three major banks. Indeed, it has been claimed that this return to concentration merely marked a *de jure* return, as *de facto* the banks had retained the centralised structure they had possessed throughout German history. Similarly, I. G. Farben and Krupp were soon back in their pre-eminent role in the German economy, in spite of the determination of the war-time allies to break up these firms so closely associated with the Nazi régime. Pehaps the greatest political success of the Confederation of German Industries (BDI), to which we shall return later, was the drastic weakening of the laws against cartels and monopolies. Only in foreign trade, with heavy and early cuts in import duties, was the practice of social market economics evident. Even here, however, the principles of social market economics were arguably contravened by the practice in the 1960s and 1970s of leaving the Mark drastically undervalued, a policy designed to help German manufacturers both at home and overseas by keeping imports dearer and exports cheaper than they need have been.

Another problematic area is the role of the banks. Although it might be excessive to say that the German banks have supplied the integrative and planning role abjured by government in West Germany, the banks do indeed play a vital role. Unlike British banks, German banks are closely involved with manufacturing industry, supplying a major portion of investment capital in exchange for stocks and seats on the supervisory boards of firms. The Deutsche Bank for example, actually owned 25 per cent of the stock of Mercedes Benz until 1975 when it extended its holding to 56 per cent. In general, banks hold 33 per cent of the seats for non-employees on the supervisory boards of West Germany's 318 largest companies. In turn, the largest companies hold seats on the boards of the banks. German bankers are apparently conscious of having a particular responsibility for the maintenance of the social and economic order, and for the harmonious functioning of the economy *Ordnungsfaktor*.

Whatever the reality, the ideology of the social market economy served several functions. Its stress on decentralisation and competition helped to differentiate West Germany from Nazi Germany, and to reduce the fears of the resurgence of German industry which were bound to arise. Above all, the social market economy provided the centre-right in Germany with an appealing ideology with which to compete against the socialists. The social market economy was established as doctrine by the dominance of the Christian Democrats throughout the 1950s and the first half of the 1960s. But the doctrine of the social market economy also helped achieve this period of centre-right dominance by blunting criticisms from the Social Democrats that the Christian Democrats were heartless conservatives, indifferent to the needs of the poor and dominated by big business. The stress on the free market economy was indeed appealing to German business, while the stress on social responsibility and social programmes helped maintain the Christian Democrats' grip on the working-class Catholic vote vital for their chances of electoral victory.

In spite of its successes over the previous thirty years, however, the West German economy looked far from healthy in the 1980s. Although West Germany had been more successful than Britain or France in restraining inflation, unemployment reached levels unprecedented since the years immediately following the Second World War, and acute fears were expressed about the ability of industries such as the car industry to survive competition from Japan.

In fact, the really high levels of economic growth of the 1950s had been declining throughout the 1960s; the economic miracle lost much of its glitter long before the crisis of the 1980s. The age of machinery in West Germany increased gradually, and the workforce also became less willing to make enormous sacrifices. Indeed, German workers were regarded, if not acquiring the worst habits of British workers, at least as having a greater fondness for leisure than their predecessors (or, as social scientists put it, as having 'post-materialist' values).

As the economic miracle ran out of steam, so did pressures increase for a new approach to economic policy. These pressures were also associated with the end of the period of Christian Democratic dominance. The 'Grand Coalition', in which the Social Democrats made their entry into the government of the Federal Republic in partnership with the Christian Democrats, made moves towards increased government planning, so popular at that time in Europe because of the apparent success of the French example. By· its very nature, the Grand Coalition was more difficult to co-ordinate than previous governments.There had been a growing awareness in the previous Christian Democratic government, however, that the capacity of the Chancellor's office to co-ordinate the work of the different ministries was inadequate. Ministries had a clear tendency – as in so many countries shown at its most extreme by the Agriculture Ministry – to develop 'clientelistic' relations with the beneficiaries of the programmes they administered. The coal industry, too, was highly subsidised by an indulgent parent ministry. Such pressures for greater co-ordination from within government combined with the concern aroused by the decline of the economic miracle to push the Coalition towards greater planning.

The 1967 Law for the Stability and Development of the Economy marked the high point of this movement. The purpose of the law was to provide for both more co-ordination within government and more co-operation between government and outside major economic interests. The interests which the framers of the law had in mind were primarily the unions and employers. The law provided that each November a forecast of economic conditions would be presented by a committee of five experts; the forecast was to inform the decisions of employers and unions as well as government in deciding what price increases or wage demands were justified. The fact that government, unions and employers would be acting on the basis of shared, agreed informaton and after mutual consultation, would, it was hoped, ensure that the decisions of the participants would be easily reconciled.

It is generally agreed, however, that attempts at planning in West Germany have not been particularly successful. The General Economic Framework Planning provided for in the 1967 Act has not had the force which most of its advocates expected. An important reason for this was that, though German unions have greater coherence and simpler structures than do unions in Britain, they were still unable to play the role which had been hoped for in reducing wage pressure during periods of full employment. This was particularly true in the boom years up to 1974. Pressure for wage increases from union members exceeded the capacity of union leaders to exert restraint in line with the agreements reached with government and employers through tripartite consultation: 'It became obvious that in a growing economy the union leadership did not possess the necessary support of its membership in keeping wage demands within the framework of the guidelines sketched by the federal government'.[4] Only in the aftermath of the first oil crisis of 1973 did the framework created by the 1967 law come close to being a forum for the making of decisions (as opposed to the recognition of changes which the participants could not fully control), a contrast with the actual decision-making powers of such bodies in the more corporatist countries. Throughout the 1970s, moreover, the pressures on the Social Democrats from declining industries and on the Free Democrats by farmers seeking subsidies ended the opportunity for the West German government to steer the economy more positively. Government expenditure on the economy became a response more to pressure than to the analysis of industrial possibilities. In all events, the principles of social market economics had been left far behind.

The General Business Environment

For most of the period since the Second World War, it has been common to hold up West Germany as the exemplar of an ideal business environment in Europe. Good labour relations, stable government and an electoral system which ensured that governments could be formed only with the support of the centrist Free Democrats, except in the most exceptional circumstances, contrasted vividly with the British experience, and seemed to help to explain the contrasting economic records of the two countries. The Social Democratic Party took in its 1957 Bad Godesburg programme a step which the British Labour Party could not: it formally accepted that its most important goals – such as greater equality of incomes, a welfare state and greater equality of opportunity – could be achieved within a capitalist framework; state ownership of industry was no longer seen as essential. Both the political and union leaderships of the German working class thus demonstrated a willingness to operate within a capitalist framework.

Such moderation had not always been a feature of German working-class movements. Germany had been one of the very first countries to develop a working-class movement, the country to which Marx, Engels and most revolutionary socialist leaders had looked for the realisation of their dreams. In the 1920s and early 1930s during the Weimar Republic the Communist Party had indeed enjoyed widespread support amongst working-class voters. Even after the Second World War, the German public was shown in opinion polls to have a greater distrust of business executives than did the British. Though the economic miracle has attenuated such suspicions, the rise of the Greens, and, in a very different way, the creation of the Bader-Meinhof gang, demonstrate the continuing radical potential of German society.

The very favourable business climate of West Germany since 1945 is therefore something which has not existed continuously throughout German history. On the contrary, German history has inclined employers to accept the need for organisation in the face of strong unions and a high degree of class consciousness manifested through the unions or support for socialist or communist parties. Whatever the position today, Germany historically was not, like the USA, a country in which employers could imagine that their mutual interests would go unchallenged.

The German political culture has always been one geared to functional representation. Going back into medieval times there has been a tradition of guilds and chambers of commerce, of *Kammern* which represented workers, farmers, merchants, etc. The combination of this tradition and class conflict has ensured that both employers and workers today are highly organised. Over 70 per cent of all but the smallest-scale German employers belong to the relevant trade association and through it the confederation of German Industries, the BDI. A parallel organisation, the BDA, was created to handle labour relations, leaving the BDI to concentrate on political affairs.[5].

Methods of Business Representation

The West German political system as a paraliamentary system has several parallels with Britain. In particular, the balance of power between the legislature and executive is tilted fairly firmly in favour of the latter. The fact that most governments have been coalitions has contributed to a lesser degree of co-ordination and central control than is found in Britain, but the differences are of degree. As in Britain, one party, the Christian Democratic Union (CDU), is closely allied with business; the other major party, the Social Democratic Party (SDP) is more allied with the unions. To an even greater degree than in Britain, however, the pro-business party is shared with other interests. The Christian Democratic Party needs in political terms to nourish its working-class vote; religion remains an important basis for political support in Germany, where class by no means explains all. The third party, the Free Democrats (FDP), though by no means as large as the CDU, is important as the 'swing' party which can give a majority to either the CDU or SDP. Fortunately for the German business community, the FDP is basically sympathetic to their interests, though more supportive of worker participation than the DBI might wish.

The fundamental strategic decisions for business in West Germany turn, therefore, on the degree to which it should concentrate on working through the Christian Democrats and the extent to which it should attempt to function as a non-partisan, technocratic lobby able to work with governments of any ideological complexion.

There is no doubt that the CDU have benefited considerably from the support of German industry. In financial terms alone, the CDU has received over 60 per cent of its funds from business. The relationship is not purely financial, however; it is also personal. The relationship between Adenauer, the first federal Chancellor, and Berg, the first leader of the BDI, was extremely close. About 10 per cent of the members of the Parliament (the Bundestag) are business executives, and they are overwhelmingly members of the CDU. In short, there is no doubt that members of the business community identify with the CDU and feel that 'their' party is in power when the CDU is in office.

Like the British business community, however, German business executives cannot afford to be so identified with the CDU that they have no way of influencing an SDP-led government. German trade associations and the BDI maintain large lobbying organisations, therefore, which are designed to ensure that the voice of business will be heard, whatever the government of the day. Some of this lobbying effort is targeted on the Bundestag. The BDI will try to ensure that all members of the Bundestag are aware of its views on controversial issues. However, it is inevitable that the BDI should find the most attentive audiences in the CDU and FDP, rather than the SDP. The FDP can be a useful counter-weight to the labour element within the CDU – being, for example, more willing to cut social expenditure for economic management reasons than the working-class element within the CDU. The Bundestag also has a well-developed committee system. Employers' organisations will therefore concentrate their attention on the leading members of the key committees rather than on the ordinary members of the Bundestag.

It is inevitable, however, that in the German parliamentary system, with effective party discipline, the real decisions should be made inside the bureaucracy and by ministers rather than on the floor or in the committees of the Bundestag. The trade associations and the BDI find, therefore, that their most effective work is done in dealing with the ministries whose work concerns them than with the Bundestag. As the trade associations and BDI have the reputation for employing high-calibre staff, they have little difficulty in securing an attentive hearing from the civil servants concerned. Indeed, close relations are fostered not only by the constant interaction between officials of the employers' organisations and the relevant civil servants but by the fact that early in their careers officials of the pressure groups are seconded to ministries (and vice-versa). Close consultation and mutual respect are normal features of the civil servant–employers' organisation relationship.

As would be the case in most countries, relationships between ministries and pressure groups differ in intensity. The BDI has a closer relation with the Ministry of Trade than with the Ministry of Finance. These links, in turn, are closer than with the Ministry of Labour, whose ties to unions are better than its ties to business. As in most countries, too, the ministry will feel that it has a responsibility to the pressure group to represent its views in dealings with other departments. The BDI can also expect access to the federal Chancellor himself. The first head of the BDI, Berg, saw Adenauer very frequently, and Adenauer would invite himself to the BDI's conferences. On one celebrated occasion, Adenauer publicly reproved two of his ministers who had displeased the BDI by disagreeing with its policies. Relations between the BDI and

Adenauer's successors were not as cordial. Erhard had displeased the BDI by taking the competitive, free-market aspects of the social market philosophy too seriously, and naturally Social Democratic Chancellors Brandt and Schmidt were closer to the unions than to management. However, the prestige of the DBI and the appreciation of socialist as well as CDU Chancellors of the dependence of the German economy on the success – especially in export markets – of its major firms ensure that the organisation will gain a respectful hearing from any Chancellor. In a perhaps perverse manner, the BDI is likely to benefit as an organisation from the rise of its opponents. The success of the Greens and the drift to the left in the SDP in opposition will convince German businessmen that they need strong organisations to represent their interests.

Several aspects of the West Geman situation might have seemed highly conducive to the creation of a neo-corporatist economy. Both business and labour have 'peak' organisations which enjoy great prestige and authority, and which have a virtual monopoly on the representation of the collective interests of their potential members. The German parliamentary system and disciplined political parties also allow government sufficient authority to make feasible tripartite bargaining between employers, unions and government. The German political culture legitimises functional representation through economic interest groups to a degree which would not be true in, say, the USA. Yet, in spite of all these advantages, the development of neo-corporatism in West Germany has been far more limited than in such neighbouring countries as Austria and the Netherlands.

A number of factors explain this situation. Undoubtedly a major factor has been the market-orientated economic strategy set, and by and large followed, by governments of the federal republic since Adenauer. The governments most likely to enter into neo-corporatist arrangements are those which have a need for the co-operation of major economic groups because they are engaged in planning (as in France) or, more commonly, because they are following a centrally-administered incomes policy. The commitment to a market economy made by West Germany in the 1950s has been attenuated by the need to assist declining industries in the 1970s. Yet the West Germans did not in practice, as we have seen, establish a truly tripartite pattern of policy-making. The movement in the direction of more corporatist forms of policy-making embodied in the 1967 Law for the Stability and Development of the economy had but limited success.

Part of the reason for the limited development of tripartism was that the West German peak associations did not have quite the authority which they had seemed to enjoy. We have seen that the unions were not able to impose limited wage increases on their members in a tight labour market to the degree which had been hoped. The BDI, too, was not immune from challenges to its authority. As early as the 1950s Berg had been rebuffed openly and vigorously by large firms which, contrary to his wishes, had wanted to participate in East–West trade. The BDI also suffered from the fact that its authority was confined to the political sphere; another organisation (the BDA) was responsible for matters concerning wage negotiations with the unions. Government itself has not enjoyed the cohesion (or, in some respects, power) desirable to make a neo-corporatist system work effectively. Apart from the constraints imposed by the nature of coalition government and the tendency for ministries to adopt clientelistic relations with interest groups that we have already discussed, the federal government lacks a number of important economic powers. The central bank (the Bundesbank) enjoys real autonomy from the federal government in the making of monetary policy. Perhaps even more important has been the fact that tax revenue in West Germany is divided between the federal government and the states (Länder), according to a complicated and relatively inflexible formula. The capacity of the federal government to steer the economy by the use of varying tax rates has thus been considerably reduced, preventing one of the basic weapons of economic planning being deployed. In a sense, therefore, West German governments are making a virtue of necessity in carrying out limited economic planning, which in turn has reduced the incentive for the government to enter into neo-corporatist relations with the major economic interest groups. In brief, the nature of the federal constitution imposes important limitations on the capacity of the federal government to implement the sort of bargain which might be expected from it by the major economic groups in any tripartite negotiations.

Conclusions

Business groups have operated in a relatively favourable environment in West Germany. They have showed, too, a capacity for solving to their satisfaction the practical problems which have arisen. In spite of the heavy emphasis on competition in social market ideology, the large firms and cartels more congruent with German economic traditions were able to re-establish themselves. Laws on competition and the prevention of monopoly were adapted to remove the strongest objections of the business community (making them, however, more acceptable to the large corporations). The law on worker participation, too, has been maintained in a form which does not overly impinge on management prerogatives. Employers have also been able to secure exchange-rate policies which have resulted in the 1960s and 1970s in the under-pricing of their exports and over-pricing of imports, in spite of the great international pressures exerted on West Germany to shrink the trade surpluses it generally enjoyed in the post-war period.

West Germany industry will face major political problems in the 1980s. Though undoubtedly still the strongest of the European economies, West Germany, like most of the European economies, faces severe competition from lower-cost or more efficient economies. The need to close down uneconomic factories, mines and railways will raise strong political protest. The SDP and unions will resist cuts in the welfare services which add (through social security contributions) to the already high cost of West German labour. The rise of the Greens, meanwhile, and the strong environmentalist sentiment on which they draw, will probably result in a strengthening of the environmental laws and regulations in West Germany, probably adding further to the costs of German industry. German labour relations, too, have been less placid in recent years than in the past. In 1984 a severe strike afflicted the car industry, important in both its size and as a symbol of West German industrial might. The strike was over demands for a 35 hour week, a proposal which will add further to the cost disadvantages of German employers. Meanwhile, the left of the SDP has been more vociferous than for many years. The economic problems of high unemployment and decreased competitiveness, and the threat to West German industries, such as shipbuilding and cars from the Far East, add to the apprehensiveness of German employers. It is likely, therefore, that they will maintain (or add to) the high levels of organisation which they have maintained. West Germany will probably remain the non-corporatist country with the best-organised employers.

4

Business and Politics in Britain

Britain has been labelled a capitalist, socialist and corporatist political system. These contradictory labels used by different writers sometimes reveal more about the attitudes of the writers than they do about Britain. However, the fact that Britain can be described in such varying ways does highlight an important fact about the country. Different tendencies do exist in Britain which can, for example, tilt policy-making in a more or less corporatist direction as governments consult more or less closely with economic groups. A temporary strengthening of a trend can lead, perhaps too easily, to articles in the press proclaiming that Britain is now, for example, a corporatist country. However, one of the features of the business–government relationship in Britain is, indeed, its flexibility. As we shall see, the degree to which government consults with the organisations representing business or labour in general varies considerably, as does the extent to which governments attempt to plan the economy.

The General Business Environment

Richard Rose has shown that the British give 'two and one half cheers' for the market economy.[1] Socialism produces more favourable responses than capitalism amongst the British in the abstract: socialism evokes more favourable and fewer unfavourable responses as an abstract doctrine than does capitalism. But when the British are asked to make judgements about the real world rather than abstract doctrines, socialism is overwhelmingly rejected, an interesting inversion of the situation in the USA. Only 5 per cent of Rose's sample wanted all industry to be owned and controlled by the government, and only another 13 per cent wanted the government to be involved in the 'day to day planning of companies'. A private enterprise system 'with enough government controls to curb abuses' or with 'a minimum of government regulation' attracted the support respectively of 39 per cent and 38 per cent of Rose's sample.

In the USA, the public was much attracted to capitalism in the abstract and favoured stronger government action in practice. In Britain, a substantial proportion of the public (though still a minority) favoured socialism in the abstract, but in more practical terms socialist measures were overwhelmingly rejected.

This apparent paradox – that many people in Britian distrust capitalism but distrust socialism in practice even more – has many parallels in politics and policy in Britain. The Labour Party, pledged by its constitution to bring in fully-blown socialism, has formed governments which enjoyed clear working majorities in Parliament from 1945–51, 1966–70, and governments with slender majorities or no overall majority from 1921–2, 1929–31, 1964–6 and 1974–9. Yet not only is there not a socialist society in Britain, but the precentage of industry in government ownership, the proportion of gross national product (GNP) spent by government and the amount of personal income taken by taxation in Britain are about average by European standards, and are actually lower than in some European countries such as France, where avowedly socialist parties have been in power for much shorter periods.[2] Although debate on the topic still continues, it is probably the case that income has not been significantly shifted to the poorest by government policies since the second World War, although the share of wealth held by the top 5 per cent has fallen. Neither has any legislation been adopted (or even proposed) which would limit fundamentally the authority of managers within their companies, or which would diminish the freedom of managers to make major decisions on, say, investment affecting their enterprises to compare with Swedish legislation conferring shares on union-run pension funds or German legislation on consultative committees. The reality of an avowedly socialist party in power has been much less fearsome than might have been supposed.

There are a number of reasons for this. One of the most important is that the Labour Party, no matter what its constitution said, has been only partly a socialist party for most of its history. The party was much more clearly influenced by unions, which provide the overwhelming majority of the party's funds, cast the majority of votes at its annual conference, and have the largest share (40 per cent) of the votes in the electoral college which chooses the leader of the Labour Party (the constituency parties and Labour MPs each have 30 per cent of the vote in the electoral college).

The domination of the Labour Party by unions is only part of the strength of unions in Britain. Just under half the British workforce is unionised; though this proportion is much higher than the proportion in France or the USA, it is lower than in many other European countries. The unions are, however, sufficiently strong in the workplace to impede management significantly and were strong enough politically until 1979 to prevent the permanent intervention of the state fundamentally to change the balance of power between management and unions. British employers have proved sufficiently incapable over the years of resisting inflationary wage claims that incomes policies (government intervention in wage bargaining to curb such wage increases) have been introduced by every government – Conservative and Labour – presiding over periods of full employment. Moreover, the productivity of British unionised workers, for example in the car industry, has often lagged far behind the productivity of identically-constructed plants operated by the same company in Europe.[3]

An influential school of thought contends that industry in Britain is held in low esteem and that, in consequence, British management is of a lower calibre than in competing countries. If true, such a theory might explain the inability of British management to cope with their highly-unionised workforce.[4] It should be noted that, contrary to general belief, British unions are not extraordinarily militant in terms of their strike record. Britain, in terms of the number of days lost because of strikes per 1000 workers, is usually about in the middle of the league table of industrial countries. Yet, unable to contain wages or control working conditions through their own efforts, many managers have looked to the state for assistance. Even with the constant changes in employment law, the power of unions within the Labour Party has so far sufficed to prevent any permanent diminution in their powers. Legislation which would have lessened the powers of unions was introduced in 1968 by the Labour Government, only to be withdrawn under union pressure. Stronger legislation was introduced by the 1970 Heath government, enacted, turned into a dead letter by the unions' defiance of the law, and repealed by the second Wilson government (1974–6).[5] The Thatcher government (since 1979) has had several measures enacted which unions feel diminish their powers. Whether the Labour party has reached such a low point that these laws will be on the statute book permanently remains to be seen. In the early 1980s it seemed that the Conservatives' laws had a better chance of being accepted by the unions than previous attempts while a majority Labour Government seemed a distant prospect.

Just as unions have looked to the Labour Party for assistance, so have most executives looked to the Conservative Party. The vast majority of business executives in Britain support the Conservative Party; the party has also benefited from donations from companies. Unlike the situation in the USA, companies in Britain are allowed to make payments to political parties from their general funds. The importance of such donations and 'in kind' contributions (such as poster space donated by the brewing industry) has been very significant to the Conservative Party. It is claimed that such contributions account for a diminishing proportion of party funds and that the proportion of funds raised by the branches of the Conservative Party through their fund-raising efforts amounts to about two-thirds of total receipts. It is even contended that the image of an affluent Conservative Party riding roughshod over a Labour Party inadequately funded by the unions and desperately poor Liberals and Social Democrats is a myth.[6] The Conservative party, such writers argue, has comparatively little money in the bank. The party can afford to have small reserves, however, because of its ability to raise money quickly. As in the 1983 election campaign, large companies and their executives will come speedily to the aid of the Conservative party when the need arises. The financing of parties in Britain is under-studied, and still partially secret, but however dependent on business they are the Conservatives remain to an important degree in terms of their support and policies the party of business.

The Conservatives are not exclusively the party of the business, however. In electoral terms, the party can win only by attracting lower-middle and working-class votes, as well as the votes of business executives and professionals. The party at the élite level is not a monolithic business party, either. The 'landed interest' of farmers and landowners has been tremendously powerful in the party in the past and remains quite strong today. Above all, the British business world is divided (and we shall have much more to say about this) not only between big and small business but between finance capital and manufacturing. It is finance capital – 'the City', as it is known – which has the closer links with the parliamentary Conservative Party. Conservative MPs such as Edward du Cann are members of firms in the City; the numerous lawyers who are Conservative MPs also have closer links with the City than with the manufacturing industry.

It is tempting to link trends in Conservative policy to trends in the composition of the parliamentary Conservative Party. The decline in the strength of the landed interest in the party and, for that matter, the decline in the percentage of the party who are former officers in the armed services seems to match a trend away from a paternalistic Conservatism and towards a harder, more ruthless investment banker of the world, mirroring the rise in the importance of the City in the parliamentary party. It is surely remarkable that the heavy toll which the recession has taken on the manufacturing industry and small businesses has aroused such little sympathy in the parliamentary party. The rise of the City interests in the party (who suffered not at all from the high interest rates and exchange rates which devastated many manufacturing firms in the early 1980s) is part of the explanation. Moreover, the rise of the professional, London-based MP has reduced even further the influence of local business executives, often the bedrock of local constituency parties.

Business Organisation and the State

Business in the USA, as we have seen, can be described as disorganised, but secure. British business looks less secure, but is it much better organised?

Compared with business in the USA, British business is well organised and closely linked to government. The CBI is clearly recognised as the spokesman for the manufacturing industry by government, even though the more right-wing Institute of Directors is on close terms with individual conservatives. It nominates representatives to the National Economic Development Council (NEDC), is listened to respectfully by Chancellors of the Exchequer before they finalise their budgets, and on questions of general economic policy.[7] The CBI nominates representatives to numerous consultative committees established by the government, and nominates members of the Health and Safety Commission which draws up regulations for workplace safety and health, and of the Manpower Services Commission which controls training policies. The CBI is accepted by the media as *the* voice of British industry, just as the TUC is accepted as the voice of British labour. The Director of the CBI is able to obtain copious coverage of statements on policy, whilst the annual conference of the CBI is given extensive live coverage by television. The CBI provides government with much useful technical advice, including a survey of wage settlements and investment plans made by its members – information of great use in economic planning.

Yet the CBI has its limitations. It has very little authority over its members, and can only urge them to follow a course of action agreed with the government. The CBI is vulnerable to the defection of large firms who are members if they are displeased with its policies. Too 'confrontational' a line with a Labour Government can embarrass the nationalised industries which are members of the CBI; too confrontational an approach to a Conservative Government, no matter how justified, leads to threats from the more doctrinaire Conservative business executives to lead their companies out of the CBI, something which happened after the Director of the CBI had threatened a 'bare knuckle fight' with the Thatcher government over its policies in 1981.

The closeness of the CBI to ministers and civil servants, whether the Conservatives or Labour is in power, is obviously the organisation's greatest asset. Officials of the CBI and senior civil servants are in daily, sometimes hourly, contact on a wide range of issues. Yet this relationship creates both opportunities for and limitations on the organisation. Interest groups wishing to enjoy close links with civil servants during the crucial period when policy options are open and ministers undecided must adhere to an unwritten Whitehall code of conduct. Confidences must be respected; leaks to the Opposition or to the press must be limited and discreet. Above all, the participation of the organisation in overt electioneering must be drastically limited. If the CBI were to campaign openly on behalf of the Conservative Party, it would soon forfeit close links with the civil service. The officials of the CBI do enjoy significant opportunities to influence civil servants because of their contact with them. Senior civil servants and CBI officials are on a first name basis – in appearance, attitudes and style they are very similar people. The price of this relationship is the necessity to avoid public campaigning. To some sections of business opinion this produces a moderation in attitude and behaviour amounting to collaboration. The Institute of Directors and Aims of Industry are two organisations which take what they see as a more vigorous stand than the CBI in defence of business interests.

The Institute of Directors, a much smaller and less technically-informed organisation than the CBI, has attempted to keep the Thatcher wing of the Conservative government true to goals such as tax cuts at the expense of government services and legislation reducing the power of unions. The Institute has strengthened its research section in recent years. Aims of Industry has launched a series of advertisements to combat what it sees as socialism and to defend capitalism. These advertisements, particularly at election time, have brought it fully into the electoral arena. For that reason, the largest (or, as Aims of Industry prefers to put it, Establishment) firms have kept away from it. The Institute of Directors enjoys very close links with certain Conservative politicians, including Margaret Thatcher; but it does not have the staff or comprehensiveness of membership seriously to challenge the CBI.

The main problem which has afflicted the CBI is that it has been able to make only very limited claims to speak on behalf of financial institutions. The City is not really part of the CBI. This gap in the comprehensiveness of the CBI's membership would cause concern *ipso facto*; the absence of the financial institutions is all the more worrying for the CBI because of the importance of financial institutions in Britain. The City, as we have seen, has particularly good contacts with the parliamentary Conservative Party and the City has other ways to influence governments of either party.[8] The City's welfare is a matter of legitimate concern to any British government because of its success in earning foreign exchange. Were it not for the success of City institutions in earning money overseas through insurance, trading and investment, the British balance of payments crises of the 1960s and 1970s would have been even deeper, and Britain almost permanently in deficit. The City has demonstrated its value as one of the few British industries to earn overseas, and to maintain its performance in spite of competition.

The City has also enjoyed special representation within government. The Bank of England has been a nationalised 'industry' since 1946. The Bank has always operated under the instructions of the government and on the government's behalf in the foreign exchange markets (for example, in defence of the pound) and in manipulating interest rates on the domestic money markets. Governors of the Bank of England have also, however, seen it as part of their duty to represent the City to the government. Governors obviously work closely with top Treasury officials and have regular access to the Chancellor of the Exchequer; Governors also have access to the Prime Minister, particularly at moments of grave crisis. In general, Governors of the Bank have been men who 'enjoyed the confidence' – that is, shared the views – of City institutions. The Bank has functioned, therefore, as a representative of financial institutions as well as a part of government.

Whether the privileged access of the City institutions to governments through the Governor provides adequate access to government for them has been doubted. Moran reports that the growing complexity of City institutions and the increasing variety of financial institutions (effectively ranging from building societies and pension funds to foreign-owned banks) has disrupted arrangements which prevailed in the past.[9] Moreover the increased use of monetary policy by both Labour and Conservative Governments since 1976 has made the Bank of England more clearly a tool of government policy than when monetary policy received less emphasis. Financial institutions may well be moving towards reliance on an organisation of their own to represent their common interests, the expansion of the scale of the Committee of London Clearing Banks being a case in point. Whatever the changes which are taking place, however, the dual role of the bank of England as part of government and representative of the City to the government has given financial institutions in the past a degree of access to ministers, particularly in financial crises, not enjoyed by the manufacturing industry.

The influence of finance capital has been strengthened further by the policies of successive governments. Both Conservative and Labour Governments have attached more or less overriding importance to the maintenance of the value of sterling against other currencies, particularly the dollar, even when market conditions have seemed to make such a defence futile. Such attempts to defend the pound gave great power to financial institutions. If the pound was very weak on the foreign exchanges, governments were forced into politically unpalatable measures such as cutting public expenditures, raising taxes and tolerating higher levels of unemployment in order to increase indirectly British competitiveness. Any slackening of resolve on the part of a government following such a course would mean that devaluation was only a matter of time. Anyone with money to spare could make more by switching their pounds into a stable or appreciating foreign currency and back again once the devaluation had occurred. Such a switching of funds (if there is a 10 per cent devaluation) yields a 10 per cent profit, minus handling fees. No commodity is as easy to move around the world as money; telephone and cable networks facilitate massive switching of funds around the world. The maintenance of confidence by governments amongst financial institutions if the currency is under pressure is vital, therefore, otherwise normal profit-maximising behaviour will bring about irresistible pressure for the devaluation the government has resisted.

Not surprisingly, therefore, once governments have set out to protect the value of the pound against pressures on the foreign exchanges, the financial institutions have exerted a major pressure on government policy. The maintenance of their confidence was essential, and nothing was more likely to destroy that confidence than policies with which the City disagreed. Expectations play a crucial role in markets, and expectations about the future value of the pound were influenced heavily by the City's opinions of government policies. This was no conspiracy; currency dealers were merely trying to maximise profits. But the opinions of financial institutions, because of their effect on the value of the pound, took on a crucial importance.

The behaviour of financial institutions during crises is in a sense but an extreme form of a general problem for Britain. The low productivity levels that British management and unions collectively have created make Britain an unattractive place for investors. British financial institutions have therefore invested heavily in competing industrialised countries as well as the Third World. This overseas investment has been seen by many as an explanation for Britain's economic failure. British industry has not had the government-inspired loans which have benefitted French industry or the close involvement of banks in firms which assist German firms undertake long-term investment projects. The Wilson Committee on the workings of financial institutions (1981) generally gave the City a clean bill of health, agreeing that there was a shortage of investment opportunities in Britain rather than a shortage of investment funds.[10] Whether *governments* could make Britain more attractive to investors, thus increasing the number of investment opportunities, and what that would mean for long-term policy on taxation, regulation and labour law, was not clear. The deleterious long-term consequences for the British manufacturing industry of investment not taking place in Britain were clearer. The whole debate over the adequacy of finance for British manufacturing industry illustrates vividly the abnormally great separation between manufacturing firms and financial institutions in Britain. Unfortunately for the CBI, which does not really speak for financial institutions (and arguably, unfortunately for the country, too), it is finance rather than manufacturing which seems the more influential in Britain.

Trade Associations

Just as it was difficult to say unambiguously how influential is the CBI, so it is equally difficult to say unambiguously what role trade associations play in British government.

Several factors aid them. First, there is a tradition in British government that government departments should consult closely with interests affected by their policies and, if possible, reach agreement on them. Policies should ideally be agreed upon, rather than imposed. Civil servants are encouraged to work closely with 'responsible' pressure group officials, particularly if they can facilitate implementation of policies by promoting compliance amongst their members, or if they can supply the traditionally non-expert British civil service with ideas, information and technical guidance.

Most trade associations are affiliated to the CBI and will try to influence government policy through it. Often, however, there will be issues on which the CBI will not wish to take a position and so the trade association will come into its own, being the only employers' voice on the subject. The CBI may wish to stay out of a debate because the topic is too specialised for a general employers' organisation, or because the topic is one on which employers are divided. The CBI would scarcely wish to offend one trade association or large firm by siding with another trade association or firm against it. The CBI is likely to stay neutral, therefore in disputes which divide its members.

Trade associations are likely to have close relations with particular government departments, or even divisions of government departments, rather than with government in general. The tradition of close consultation between government and affected interests in Britain ensures that the officials of the well-organised trade association will know personally, and will be in almost daily contact with, civil servants working on policies of importance to them. The trade associations with the most influence will be the trade associations with prestige and with appropriate technical skills. Prestige will be gained primarily through the recruitment of a high proportion of potential members. The trade association which can claim to speak for all major employers in its field, with a high 'density' of membership, will thereby acquire a degree of legitimacy which a trade association with less complete membership cannot match. Trade associations can also acquire influence through maximising their technical expertise. British civil servants, particularly in the higher reaches of the civil service, are not technical experts. Although the civil service does have economic and scientific sections within it, the civil servant will generally be appreciative of any reasonably objective analysis of the economic or scientific consequences of a proposed policy. The trade association which develops a reputation for competent analysis of policy proposals will be highly valued in Whitehall.

Like many British interest groups, trade associations will expect that once the government department with which they usually deal has consulted with the trade associations relevant to its work, its civil servants and ministers will represent their views within government. The Department of Trade and Industry at both the official and ministerial level are expected, therefore, to push the needs of industry (such as a reduction in payroll taxes) in dealing with the Treasury or other departments.

Yet the Devlin Report,[11] commissioned by the CBI on the representation of British industry, pointed to severe failings in trade associations. Generalisation was hazardous because of the considerable variation in the nature of trade associations, some being responsible for representation and labour relations, others for representation only. In some industries there was only one trade association; in other industries there was more than one. In general, however, trade associations suffered from several disabilities. First, like the CBI itself, they looked under-staffed and under-funded by continental European standards. This is not to say that they were as weak as the American trade associations described by Bauer, Pool and Dexter.[12] The trade associations were, however, less impressive in terms of budget, number of personnel and technical knowledge than might have been expected. Second, and no doubt in part because of the first factor, government departments were likely to consult individual companies, particularly the larger ones, rather than relying on the trade associations. Large firms could supply more technical information than many trade associations. In consequence, trade associations were *one* – perhaps even the major, but rarely the only – link between government and industry. The standing of trade associations was obviously less, therefore, than in countries in which all dealings between a government department and an industry are routed through the trade association.

Industrial Policy and Planning

The inconsistency of policy in Britain has been one of the large number of factors cited as contributing to her economic problems. This inconsistency in policy has been observable not only between ministries of different parties but *within* governments of the same party. Industrial policies illustrate this clearly.

After their victory in 1951 the Conservative Party set about creating a 'bonfire of controls' left from the war-time era or the period of extremely difficult transition to peace managed by the Labour government of 1945–51. With a few exceptions (such as limitations on the movement of investment funds overseas), the Conservatives returned Britain to a free-market system. Most of the industries taken into public ownership by the Labour Government (coal, gas, the railways and canals) were kept in public ownership. The steel industry, however, began its peace-time career as a political football, the Labour Party pledged to its public, the Conservatives to its private ownership (the process was more or less ended in the 1970s by the bankruptcy of the industry; no one wanted to own British Steel in the end).[13]

The existence of a nationalised sector meant that ministers could never entirely avoid industrial issues again, particularly as the industries in public ownership suffered from awkward problems of transition to new circumstances (for example, coal and the railways), often made heavy losses, and proved to be at least as prone to industrial unrest as private industry. Moreover, ministers of both parties were unable to resist the temptation to intervene in nationalised industries for political reasons. However, the buoyant world economy of the 1950s produced steady economic growth in Britain so that in the popular mind the Conservatives in the 1959 election campaign were associated with the slogan 'You've never had it so good'. The signs of comparative British decline were, however, becoming apparent as British growth rates and shares of world trade declined. By 1963, the balance of payments crises which preoccupied so much of the attention of modern British government were serious. The response of British governments to such problems since the Second World War had been to rely on macroeconomic management, eschewing detailed involvement in industry (except, for political or practical reasons, in the nationalised industries).[14] The ideas of Keynes had made a particularly deep impression in his native land; neither economists nor civil servants paid much attention to detailed industrial issues. Indeed, by background, training and temperament most civil servants had little interest in (or ability to comprehend) technical industrial issues.

The growing signs of Britain's comparative economic failure led in the early 1960s to an interest in indicative planning in which the government, in partnership with major economic groups, would set out goals for the growth of both the entire economy and specific industries. This exercise would not result in the imposition of targets or requirements on specific industries, firms or unions. The process of consultation would, however, result in the identification of potential barriers to growth, such as a shortage of steel or skilled labour, which could then be removed by government or industry (the nature of indicative planning will be discussed more fully in Chapter 5).

The movement towards indicative planning began under the Conservative government in 1962 with the creation of the NEDC (widely referred to as 'Neddy') to act as a forum for informed discussion between government, management and unions. The NEDC was subsequently followed by 'little Neddies' or Economic

Development Councils (EDCs) for specific industries. The Labour Government of 1964 went further by creating a new Department of Economic Affairs (DEA) to supervise the creation of a National Plan. The National Plan was intended to secure a high rate of economic growth, and was to be written by the DEA in consultation with unions, employers (grouped in their new umbrella organisation, the CBI) and interest groups representing other major economic groups (for example, the NFU). The DEA itself was to be a growth-orientated, strategically-minded ministry acting as a counterweight within government to the Treasury, whose concerns with short-term economic management (such as protecting the pound on the foreign exchanges or handling balance of payments crises) could easily undermine the Plan.

In fact, in spite of the high political standing of the first Secretary of State at the DEA, George Brown (then Deputy Leader of the Labour Party), the Plan was soon abandoned. The major reason for its demise was that the Labour Government, showing a deeply conservative spirit, placed the defence of the value of the pound ahead of the strategic objectives of economic growth. Tax increases and expenditure cuts removed the premises on which the Plan had been built, and ensured the supremacy of the Treasury over the DEA. After the attempt to defend the value of the pound ended in failure with its devaluation in 1967, Labour governments retained an interest in detailed intervention in the economy, but never reverted to planning. Instead, new organisations – the Industrial Reorganisation Corporation (IRC), largely independent of government, and a Ministry of Technology – sought to promote detailed changes. The IRC was to assist mergers to produce larger (and, it was hoped therefore, more efficient) firms, while the Ministry of Technology gave grants to encourage the development of more advanced products or techniques.

The Conservative victory of 1970 brought a sharp shift away from detailed intervention. *Laissez–faire* attitudes had grown within the Conservative Party during its period in opposition, away from the responsibilities of government. The Party's Leader, Edward Heath, had made his mark by steering through Parliament legislation to promote competition in the retail grocery trade: at a meeting of party leaders in a hotel at Selsdon Park, the Party's leaders endorsed a programme for less detailed government intervention in industry, more competition and legislation to regulate the unions, something the Labour Government had tried but failed to do. The IRC and Ministry of Technology were abolished and legislation providing for grants to industry for specified purposes and projects repealed. The spirit of the programme was attacked by its critics as promoting the outlook of 'Selsdon Man' a mythical creature who was either *homo economicus*, or a beast dedicated to competition whatever the social costs.

Within three years a dramatic change in policy, or 'U-turn' had taken place. There was a new Industry Act (1972) once more giving authority for government intervention in specific industries or firms. The government did not engage in full-scale planning, but did find a new interest in consultation and partnership with the CBI and TUC. The 'anti-union' legislation, so disliked by the TUC, was allowed to lapse into disuse after it had proved difficult to impose. Ironically, however, the government's new-found interventionism also led it back to the troubled waters of incomes policy, which had caused the previous Labour Government much grief in spite of its close links with the unions.

The Conservative Government fell in 1974 after failing to win an election fought amidst the economic disruption of a miners' strike which the government would neither resist vigorously nor settle on the miners' terms. The subsequent Labour Government passed through two phases. In the first, the government forged unusually close links with the TUC and, to a much lesser extent, the CBI. Assistance was given to a wide range of firms and industries and all legislation unwelcome to unions was ignored. The economic crises of British uncompetitiveness and severe balance of payments/ exchange rate crises were ignored, however. In 1976, a major crisis finally overwhelmed the pound, the International Monetary Fund (IMF) was asked for a loan, and as financial crises deepened, the government reversed policies again. The government imposed an incomes policy which in 1978–9 resulted in 'the winter of discontent' in which strikes in essential services brought disruption to the country on a scale unmatched since the miners' strike of 1973–4.

The extent to which the Thatcher Government since 1979 has changed policy can be questioned. As with its predecessors, large sums were paid to firms in financial trouble, such as British Leyland and the National Coal Board. However, once again a spirit of disengagement from detail prevailed. Attempts were made to tackle what was seen as the excessive power of unions, and many publicly-owned firms were returned to private ownership ('privatised') and assistance to firms was given reluctantly, reflecting the government's commitment to disengagement in principle if not in practice. The future of industry was generally seen as being in its own hands – or the market's. The capacity of government to influence developments was small.

All recent governments in Britain have, therefore, had some type of industrial policy. But policies have been short-lived, inconsistent and short-term. Most of the money paid to industry since 1970 – a massive amount – has gone to ease the decline of industries such as shipbuilding or steel. Comparatively little has gone into the development of growing industries which might have provided a brighter economic future for Britain.

Why has it proved so difficult to establish a more permanent and more fruitful partnership between government and industry in Britain? The answers are ideological, political and administrative.

At the *ideological* level, Britain is an unusually complex country. Britain can claim to be the home of both conservative thought (Burke) and liberalism (Mill). The strength of liberal economic thought in Britain is stressed little, but in practice is far stronger than in many industrial democracies (France and Japan, for example). Of course, the industrial revolution in Britain was not sponsored by government and was, to a greater degree than in Germany, France or Japan, the result of 'spontaneous' social, economic and technological change. In consequence, the habit of thinking of economic (especially industrial) development as something which occurs 'outside' the realm of government is deeply based in Britain. Of course, governments may influence for better or worse the prospects for growth by a variety of policies as diverse as education, labour law and (since the 1940s) Keynesian economic management. The belief that business executives have the responsibility to find and develop business opportunities is deeply rooted, however.

The *political* reasons why industrial policy is not more deeply rooted include, of course, the commitment of a large and growing part of the Conservative Party to such liberal principles. The early Heath Administration (1970) and the Thatcher Government (since 1979) both have displayed an antipathy in principle to planning or detailed intervention in the economy. A further political problem is that the competitive British party system has provided a massive incentive to governments to yield to pressure from geographically-concentrated interests. Industries like textiles, agriculture and the car industry employ large numbers in readily-identifiable areas. Within those areas, a number of parliamentary constituencies exist which are held by relatively small majorities. Policies which please car workers, farmers or textile workers might, therefore, win an election for a party. It is not surprising, therefore, that both Conservative and Labour governments have shown a readiness to adopt policies for industries as diverse as agriculture and the ports which have a political rather than economic *rationale*. Fear of such pressures has also prompted politicians and civil servants to try to avoid detailed involvement in industry. If politicians are involved in deciding where a new steel mill will be built, or which port should be developed, they will inevitably come under strong political pressures from the localities concerned. One reason for avoiding detailed involvement in industrial decisions is therefore to avoid such pressures. Many civil servants are well aware of the frequency with which politicians have bowed to such pressures, and the adverse economic consequences of doing so. Such pessimism about politicians has strengthened the general antipathy of the civil service to involvement in the details of industrial decision-making.

The *administrative* factors contributing to the hostility to planning in Britain include the nature and attitudes of the top civil servants. Partly for general cultural reasons, and partly because they can see so easily the vulnerability of British governments to strategically-located interests, the civil servants are very wary of planning or government assistance to specific industries. This tendency is reinforced by the background and ethos of the top civil service. The top civil service is disproportionately composed of arts graduates (usually from Oxford or Cambridge) who have, in their career choice, consciously repudiated industry. Only in the Ministry of Defence do top civil servants become involved in detailed industrial issues. Moreover, unlike the situation in Japan or France, there is no tradition of top civil servants moving out into top industrial management while retaining civil service links. Indeed, the few such moves which have taken place (revealingly, usually into the City rather than manufacturing) prompted allegations of corruption. The civil service in Britain, which traditionally has devolved the detailed implementation of policies to lower units of government (as in the case of education), is used to thinking in terms of applying general rules, not to handling specific cases. The giving of assistance to individual firms or industries, therefore, does not come naturally to them, involving as it does a style of administration which is the antithesis of rulebound. The incomplete coverage of the CBI in terms of membership, the division between manufacturing and finance and the under-development of many trade associations also all impede attempts at planning.

The strength of conflicting tendencies in British politics needs little emphasis either. The interventionist and socialist tendencies in the Labour Party and the acceptance of a strong role for the state by traditional Conservatives facilitate planning. The emphasis on consultation with 'legitimate' interests in the civil service and, above all, the deep problems of British industry, the failures of British management, and high levels of unemployment will make it difficult for governments to retreat permanently to the disengagement of the 1950s. It is striking that, in spite of all the potential support for planning in Britain, the industrial policies pursued have been so short-lived. There certainly remains the danger that Britain will continue to oscillate between American-style 'disengagement' and French-style 'involvement'.

Conclusions

Britain falls between two stools both in its industrial policies and in the function of its employers' associations. Policy is neither consistently *laissez-faire* nor consistently interventionist. Employers' groups are stronger, more prestigious and more closely integrated with government than those in the USA, yet compare less well in these respects with their equivalents in many industrialised democracies. Perhaps this reflects the inability to resolve major questions of political economy – such as the role of government, business and unions – which has plagued Britain for so long.

5

Government and Industry in France

Dangers for Capitalism

The survival of private enterprise in France seemed to many problematic immediately after the Second World War. The radical sentiments stirred by the war throughout Europe and, after the German attack on the Soviet Union, the prominent role of the Communist Party in the Resistance carried support for the French Communist Party (PCF) to new heights. The PCF gained 28.6 per cent of the vote in the November 1946 elections, apparently demonstrating the existence of a strong radical challenge to the capitalist order. Moreover, many French voters believed that French industrialists had been guilty of collaboration with the Germans during the Occupation, while much of the Right had been discredited in the years up to the fall of France. The *Comité National du Patronat Français* (CNPF) commissioned an opinion poll after the war on attitudes to private employers; its results were so bad from the employers' point of view that the results of the poll were suppressed.

Whatever the extent of collaboration by French employers in war-time, there was a strong argument to be made that French industrialists had failed their country before the Second World War. French industry in the inter-war period was notorious for its conservative and uncompetitive practices. Sheltering from foreign competition behind the highest tariff barriers in Europe, French employers further reduced the need to modernise or change by forming cartels to divide the domestic market between them. The employers no doubt in part merely reflected the conservatism of

French society as a whole. Though it is a study of rural France, Laurence Wylie's *Village in the Vaucluse*[1] presented a picture of a society that was conservative, non-adaptive, and pessimistic about its own future. Writers on France before the Second World War noticed such characteristics in French society in general. Economic geography textbooks, in consequence, would point to France as a country comparatively rich in natural resources but held back economically by conservatism, inefficiency and the power of special interests. (It is a picture Britons may find disturbingly reminiscent of accounts of their own country today.)

In any event, of course, private industry has not only survived in France but, until the recessions of the 1970s, both private and state-owned industry contributed to a period of sustained economic growth which took average incomes in France from far below to far above their British counterparts. France has experienced, since the 1950s, one of the highest growth rates in the world. A study in the 1970s by the American Hudson Institute forecast that France would be the richest country in Europe, apart from Sweden.[2] Although such a forecast seemed over-optimistic in the 1980s, the fact that it could plausibly be advanced illustrated the enormous change in France since the Second World War.

In reality, a number of factors, including this remarkable increase in prosperity, reduced the danger for capitalism in France. The PCF was 'ghettoised'. Tainted by expansion of Soviet power in Europe – often, as in Czechoslovakia, at the expense of democracy – and by its slavish devotion to Soviet foreign policy, the PCF steadily lost ground in the electorate. The PCF's share of the vote fell back to around one-fifth of the electorate by 1968, and then declined even further in the late 1970s to 16.2 per cent in 1981. Moreover, until the rejuvenated Socialist Party was prepared to deal from a position of strength, with the Communist Party forming a coalition with it in 1980 which captured the presidency and Parliament, other political parties were not prepared to deal with the PCF. Writing of his post-war government, de Gaulle remarked that he could not give the Foreign Ministry to a Communist minister for fear of endangering France, and he could not give the Ministry of the Interior to a Communist either since it guarded the Foreign Ministry. The Communist seizures of power in Eastern Europe in the 1940s naturally strengthened such fears of the PCF, perhaps the Communist Party most obedient to Moscow outside Eastern Europe. In consequence, the Left was split between democratic socialists and a PCF which was beyond the pale.

The divisions on the Left in France are all the more important because of their consequences for French unions. Unions in France are not strong in general. Only 20 per cent of the workforce can be regarded as members of unions in the British or American sense of paying dues regularly in order to hold a union card. This weakness is accentuated by the split between Communist, Socialist and the formerly Catholic affiliated *Force Ouvrière*. The distrust of the Communist Party which impeded co-operation between Socialists and Communists politically weakened the chances of co-operation between the unions industrially. In consequence, French managers have not had to worry about the institutionalised power of labour at the factory level which has confronted British managers. This is not to say that industrial relations in France have always been smooth. On the contrary, French labour has periodically displayed a potential for almost revolutionary action rarely matched in Europe. In 1968, the protests of students in Paris unleashed a wave of strikes and factory occupations which rocked the Republic; only after de Gaulle had secretly visited French troops in Germany to assure himself of their loyalty and availability to suppress insurrection did he recover his nerve. But, as in similar circumstances in the 1930s, though workers made considerable immediate gains (for example, in wage increases), there was no translation of this semi-revolutionary upheaval into institutionalised union power.

It was true that there was a consensus in governing circles more conducive to nationalisation, especially in the immediate post-war years, than in Britain (let alone the USA). In consequence, France acquired a public sector larger than in most European countries. About 11 per cent of the workforce in France today is employed in state-owned enterprises, a figure about 50 per cent higher than in Britain or Italy. The state owns not only industries commonly nationalised – gas, electricity and the railways – but also aircraft construction, the Renault car manufacturers and, since 1981, the banks. The nationalised industries have themselves acquired subsidiaries, so that a number of firms not formally nationalised are nonetheless state-owned. (One example, ironically, is the American Motors Corporation in the USA, itself set against 'socialisation'.) However, most industries are still privately owned, and though the French Right does not have the antipathy to nationalisation found amongst British or American conservatives, the immediate post-war consensus in favour of nationalisation which grew out of the Resistance has dissipated.

One might argue, then, that threats to capitalism in general in France have been contained better than employers could have hoped in 1946. Divisions on the Left have helped in this process. It should also be emphasised, however, that in France social class is not the only determinant of political allegiance. Practising Catholics have tended to vote for conservative parties because the Left in France has been not only socialist but also anti-clerical. The dual division of France on the grounds of religion *v.* anti-clericalism – and on the grounds of social class – helped to stabilise what for business had seemed a dangerous situation.

Organisation of Business

French culture is not as favourably disposed to interest groups as is American or even British culture. The very term 'interest group' is used by civil servants as a term of opprobrium. An interest group to them is necessarily a self-interested group whose claims detract from the public good. The public, too, has often been thought of as having an ambivalent attitude to interest group activity. De Tocqueville argued that the French had two conflicting attitudes towards author-ity, one supporting authoritarian rule by distant rulers, the other inclining them to revolt against their rulers.[3] Neither practice is conducive to the growth of institutionalised interest groups.

At first glance, however, French industry seems highly organised politically. The *Comité National du Patronat Français* (CNPF) provides an umbrella organisation for the collective interests of French employers. In practice, however, there are doubts about its strength. This is not only because it is challenged by a shriller organisation, the *Syndicat National des Producteur Industriels* (SNPI), but because of the breadth of its coverage. Like all peak or umbrella organisations, the CNPF finds that the maintenance of unity involves striking a very delicate balance between component industries. The decentralisation of influence within the CNPF is considerable and has irritated French government which, like governments or politicians everywhere, sometimes hopes to find a unified voice for business as a whole – if only to legitimate policies it had already planned to follow. The CNPF, after all, is a coalition of trade associations; individual firms cannot join. The government therefore encouraged a reorganisation of the CNPF in 1969 which was designed to increase the power of its leaders. The CNPF is still generally associated, however, with large-scale enterprises; it is this which has fuelled the desire for the existence of a separate organisation for small-scale enterprises. Moreover, the CNPF does not by any means monopolise business representation in France. It has been calculated that only one-fortieth of expenditure on representation of business interests by firms goes to the CNPF.[4] It is governed by an Executive Council dominated by the leaders of trade associations representing the major industries (such as the textile, car, oil and chemical industries) which pay most of the CNPF's costs. Hayward reports, however, that although the CNPF is most trusted by the largest Paris-based firms, the smaller, provincial firms are still much more likely to believe that the CNPF accurately represents them than not.[5] The CNPF thus retains widespread legitimacy in business circles.

There are also numerous trade associations in France. As in Britain, their quality varies considerably. There has been a tendency, however, for the trade associations to increase in strength *vis-à-vis* individual firms. Zysman reports, for example, that the proportion of seats held on consultative committees by trade associations, as opposed to individual firms, has increased considerably.[6] Some of the trade associations have developed only because of the deliberate or accidental support of the state. The Vichy régime obliged firms to belong to trade chambers, thus accustoming them to paying subscriptions.[7] The fact that France has had what Hayward has called a 'semi-permanent' incomes policy has encouraged firms to join interest groups in the quest for extra leverage with government on matters of crucial concern to any enterprise.[8] The Chambre Syndicale de la Siderurgie Française (CSSF), the trade association for the steel industry, in contrast to the trade associations in less-organised industries, has a history going back to the mid-nineteenth century. The CSSF is so powerful *vis-à-vis* individual firms that it guides their strategies and arranges joint borrowing. Apart from representing the industry to the National Assembly and executive, the CSSF provides its members with extensive services, including comparative cost studies, centralised purchasing of inputs and research.

The style of trade associations and the CNPF is generally technocratic. Wilson quotes one of the trade association leaders he interviewed as arguing for a technocratic approach: 'We try to avoid political discussion because this tends to become polemic rather than produce constructive debate.'[9] There is a tendency for trade associations to have a dual leadership: a president who is popular with (or at least acceptable to) the membership and a more technically-minded director-general.[10] Many of the directors-general of trade associations are examples of a more general phenomenon in France known as *pantouflage*, the process of civil servants taking jobs in organisations and firms they have dealt with. The presence of these technicians in the highest posts of trade associations is an indication of the closeness of the ties between trade associations and government departments. Hayward reports that the closeness of trade associations to the relevant ministry is so great that divisions within trade associations more or less correspond to divisions within the ministry.[11]

Planning

The organisation of business interest groups in France is not particularly unusual. The CNPF is perhaps more authoritative than employers' 'umbrella' organisations in most countries. The most distinctive feature of business–government relations is the broader government–industry relationship.

France was one of those countries to which the industrial revolution came late. In 1900, France still was a rural country with pockets of industry, unlike the situation in Britain in which the vast majority of the population lived in urban industrial centres. This alone might have inclined the French towards a more activist role: the countries which industrialised late and which therefore had 'infant industries' to protect were in general less inclined to follow a *laissez-faire* approach in economic policy. In France, however, this general tendency was strengthened by traditions of centralisation and government intervention stretching back to the seventeenth century. Indeed, it can be argued that protectionism and government intervention to assist in the development of specific industries are much more common in French history than periods of *laissez-faire* or free trade. We have noted how considerable was the protection of French industry by tariffs between the two World Wars; such protectionism is probably more common in French history than the greater (but not complete) stress on freer trade since 1960.

It is not surprising, therefore, that when the French élite began to consider how to rebuild France after the Second World War, they should have accepted the need for government involvement and even leadership. The 'spirit of the Resistance' again helped to legitimate the idea that government should concert industrial development on behalf of the nation. The result was a series of Five-year Plans, themselves the product of extensive consultation between government, unions and industry. The French are now (1984) in the period of the eighth of the Five-year Plans. The Plans have had a very different character, however. Whereas the first Plan was very much concerned with the allocation of strategic but scarce resources, such as building materials or steel, the most recent Plans have been more statements of aspirations, often of a political character (dealing with topics such as the balance between production and social expenditure).[12] As the French economy has become more open to the influence of international factors due to an increased reliance on exports and (because of the General Agreement on Tariffs and Trade (GATT) and the EEC) a diminished ability to restrict imports, the capacity of the French to plan their economy has necessarily diminished.

French planning has always been *indicative*. That is to say, French planning has always in principle merely *indicated* lines of possible growth and development. Firms have not been obliged to follow the Plan, or to pursue goals consistent with it. Indicative planning is thus not the same as centralised planning: it is rather something of a 'middle way' between a free market and centralised planning. Its advantages lie supposedly not only in the discovery of potential lines of development for the economy in general but in the co-ordination of the plans of different industries. An anticipated increase in demand for agricultural machinery thus allows the steel industry to develop the capacity to produce the type of steel required for such machinery; 'bottlenecks' in the economy or the need to import can thereby be avoided.

Plans are the product of an elaborate exercise in consultation.[13] The government, through the *Commissariat du Plan*, provides economic forecasts; working parties involving civil servants, representatives of unions and employers meet to discuss objectives and prospects for industrial sectors, and the *Commissariat du Plan* marries the results of these sector groups with the government's economic forecasts. The resulting Plan is therefore, in theory, the product of consultation between the government and the 'social partners' of labour and capital. The legitimacy of the Plan is further ensured by its endorsement by the Parliament.

Whether the planning exercise or the Plan itself ever had quite the status they enjoyed on paper can be questioned. There is general agreement that French unions were in practice much less influential than the formal descriptions of the planning process would seem to suggest. Shonfield concluded that French planning 'relied essentially on the close contacts established between a number of like-minded men in the civil service and in big business. Organised labour, small business and, most of the time, the ministers in the government of the day were largely passed by.'[14] In perhaps the most detailed empirical study of French planning, MacArthur and Scott concluded that at the heart of it was 'a close relationship between business and the state'.[15] Cohen similarly concluded that 'The *économie concerté* is a partnership of big business, the state and, in theory though not in practice, the trade unions.'[16]

A certain degree of scepticism about the importance of the Plan itself is also justified. MacArthur and Scott found that the Plan was not a major influence on the plans of the individual firms. The government, equally, was not in practice bound to follow the Plan. There was often a fight within government, between the agencies of government which took responsibility for facilitating economic growth and those which were responsible for financial stability. The Ministry of Industry, for example, might use the Plan to press for economic growth; the officials of the Ministry of Finance might play down the importance of the Plan, even refusing to have a copy of it in their office. Politicians, in contrast, may have included in the Plan more and more of their general political beliefs and hopes.

Even if the Plan was in practice binding on neither government nor industry, it still stands as an emblem of the distinctive government–business relationship which exists in France. Both inside and outside the Plan's framework, French government has acted as the motor for the advance of the French economy. This is in part because French governments, pursuing their traditional goals of French power and influence, have seen as the means to those goals today the strengthening of the French economy. It was de Gaulle who made that point most explicitly,[17] arguing that in the contemporary world, the glory of France depended on the strength of its economy. Stanley Hoffman brought out vividly the transformation of the role of the French state. Whereas the state had expressed, protected and guaranteed a conservative static social order by granting concessions to special interest groups, it now took the lead towards greater efficiency. 'When the watchdog became a greyhound, those holding the leash had to learn to run.'[18]

French industrial policy has also not been dosed with the nostrums of classical economics. Instead of focusing on short-term profitability or regarding as axiomatically correct the decisions of the market, it has taken a much more structural view of French industry. The goal has been to ensure that France is represented in the industries of the future (space, aircraft, cars), generally by two firms. The classic example is the car industry where France, represented by the privately-owned Talbot–Peugeot and the state-owned Renault, has become one of the world's leading car manufacturers in the same period as the British car industry collapsed. The government views large firms with favour, and often gives small business the feeling that it is regarded as outmoded. The French thus do not follow the anti-monopoly practices common in the USA. On the contrary, industrial giants capable of competing in international markets are the goal.

The government has at its disposal a number of weapons for use in the pursuit of industrial policy goals. First, whatever the theory of GATT or the EEC, the French civil service has managed to impede the import of goods threatening the French industry. The Japanese car and video cassette recorders found that major administrative barriers were put in their way, unlike the situation in Britain or the USA where civil servants faithfully honoured free-trade rules. Second, the large nationalised sector of French industry joins with government itself to provide a sizeable protected market for French industry. It is inconceivable that the French air force or the government-owned airline Air France would buy military or civilian planes from the USA if a French alternative was available; the same cannot be said of the British Royal Air Force (or, when it was a state-owned airline, British Airways – which, in fact, had a strong attachment to the American planemaker, Boeing). Finally, the French government, even before the nationalisation of banks in the 1980s, had at its disposal considerable investment funds through government-controlled savings banks such as the *Caisse des Depôts*. Funds from these banks would be made available on favourable terms of interest to firms undertaking investments of which the government approved (and, of course, denied to those who did not). Government has thus had a variety of practical measures available to it to assist in the implementation of its plans for the development of French industry.

The question still arises why the concerted action of government and industry has been more prevalent and successful in France than, say, in Britain.

The most important single explanation is the nature of the French bureaucracy. At its highest levels the French bureaucracy has been disproportionately – and overwhelmingly – recruited from the École Polytechnique and the École Normal d'Administration (ENA). The most successful graduates of these bodies are admitted to the *Grands Corps* of the civil service, such as *Ponts et Chaussés*, handling civil engineering and the Inspectorate of Finances. The fact that the top civil servants are recruited from the Polytechnique and ENA has a number of important consequences. First, their élite status prepares (and predisposes) them for a leadership role in French society, particularly in economic matters. Second, the nature of their education increases their willingness – unlike the top British civil service – to take an interest in the details of individual firms and industries, and not just in macroeconomic policy. Finally, graduates of the Polytechnique are bonded together by a loyalty to each other and familiarity with their fellow graduates who so often occupy the top positions in French society.[19]

For it is the case that the graduates of the Polytechnique and ENA occupy the crucial positions in business as well as government. The process of *pantouflage* results in the movement of the very highest civil servants from government into the management of private firms, particularly the largest of the private firms. Vincent Wright reports that of the 560 firms employing more than 1000 workers, a majority were headed by a graduate of the École Polytechnique and almost all had ex-civil servants on their Boards of Directors.[20] Whereas such moves are feared in the USA and Britain as extending the influence of business into government, *pantouflage* is welcomed in France as a means of extending the influence of government into large-scale businesses. Suleiman has drawn attention to the increasing percentage of the graduates of the

École Polytechnique who resign from public service immediately after graduating and enter private industry without a civil service career.[21] But even these graduates remain a resource for the state, tied to their more numerous colleagues in the civil service by a common education and friendships. Thus, as befits its role in co-ordinating government and industry, the cohesive élite of the French civil service spans both the civil service and the highest posts in private industry.

A great danger in economic planning is that government intervention will be used to maintain inefficient doomed industries, rather than to promote new ones. Probably too much of British government expenditure on industry has gone on declining and irretrievable industries. The political pressures from those working in a declining industry can often outweigh the more general but less active interest in economic efficiency. The French interventionist state has by and large avoided the danger of being trapped into supporting primarily declining industries; even the 1981 the Socialist Mitterrand government has cut state assistance to doomed industries to a greater extent than the Conservatives in Britain have felt able to.

The reasons why the French have by and large minimised political pressures on industrial policy have varied. As we have seen, the bureaucracy has always been accorded high status in economic policy-making. Under the Fourth Republic, the power of civil servants was enhanced by the weakness of the politicians. The instability of government does not always produce turnover in the individual ministries; a politician might hold the same post in different governments. But the instability of governments, the preoccupation of politicians with staying in power and the changes which did occur in Cabinet portfolios reduced the capacity of politicians to disturb the plans of their civil servants. In contrast, the civil servants who had acquired (particularly at the ENA) a strong sense of mission had long-term goals and lengthy tenure of office in which to achieve them.

The constitution of the Fifth Republic was designed to strengthen the executive. The government was in practice led by the directly-elected president whose seven-year term of office freed him from undue concern over re-election for long periods (though President Mitterrand wants to cut the term to five years). The Parliament was reduced in power substantially. Its powers to remove Cabinets from office, or even to block government legislation, were reduced substantially. The Fifth Republic was dominated until 1973 by the followers of General de Gaulle; only since the early 1970s has there been serious inter-party competition for the presidency and parliamentary majority. This again has increased the freedom of civil servants to make policy free from overwhelming political pressures. There are, of course, interest groups which have secured special treatment from the state; farmers are a notorious example. But, in dramatic contrast to its history before the Second World War, the French state has shown greater strength than most, pushing through crucial decisions on industrial structure and development. For better or worse, the French proved able to make (and implement) decisions on topics such as airport development or ports or atomic power which their British counterparts vainly struggled with.

Of course, not all the explanation of French economic growth is to be found in the business–government relationship. The willingness of French politicians to give economic growth priority over the fight against inflation was also important. Moreover, the slowness of the French economy to develop before the Second World War meant that there were easy gains to be made by switching under-employed labour off the land or by conservative firms adopting modern techniques. Nonetheless, the business–government partnership has lain at the heart of French economic growth. The dramatic change in the mood of French industrialists from the conservative pessimism of the 1920s and 1930s to the expansionism of the 1950s, 1960s and 1970s itself requires explanation. The most plausible explanation is that it is the 'educational' activities of French planners (and, in some cases, the direct intervention of the government itself) which has made all the difference.[22]

Conclusions

Whether French government can continue to play such a positive role in the future remains to be seen, but it looks unlikely. The increased openness of the French economy to foreign competition, particularly within the EEC, reduces the opportunity for economic planning. While the early tensions between President Mitterrand's Socialist/Communist Government and the business community were eased when the government was forced by pressures on the franc to change its policies, it is still unclear what the long-term consequences of the Mitterrand Presidency will be. Planning procedures, for example, were revised considerably in 1982 to make them more democratic; whether this change is real or illusory remains to be seen. The French economy, though more lively than the British in terms of economic growth, faces the problems of inflation, declining competitiveness and high unemployment that have afflicted so many countries in the 1970s and 1980s. The attempt by Mitterand to reflate the French economy in isolation failed, showing how international trade and financial considerations could overcome the priorities of a French government. The days of autonomy in economic policy-making had passed for France, and most other countries. French industrial policy became, to a greater extent, a 'firefighting' operation, putting money into troubled as well as promising industries. The French system was thus not immune from the general questioning of economic practices produced by the economic recession of the 1970s and 1980s.

The French example also points to the inadequacy of conceptualising business – government relations purely in terms of power. Did French industry have power over the French state, or vice-versa? Certainly business was able to obtain special privileges from government, but government also steered industry in the directions it favoured. In a successful quest for increased power, prestige and wealth for France, a governmental technocracy which also reached into the large-scale private firms produced economic growth which might not have materialised if the private sector had been left to its own devices. It is traditional in Britain and the USA to think of government and industry as two separate areas which press upon each other but remain distant. Obviously in France this 'distinctness' of government and industry has not been preserved. On the contrary, French government involved itself in the details of French industrial life, not to contain or alter commercial priorities (for example, by imposing regulations to protect the environment), but by exhorting and assisting French industry to exploit commercial opportunities. Some Marxists might argue that the pattern of government-led capitalist development illustrates the dominance of both state and industry by the bourgeoisie. A more plausible interpretation which might find favour with different types of Marxists would be that the states's interests in a strong French economy and the capitalist's interests in profits coincided. The success of the state in educating French entrepreneurs into being more successful served both their interests.

6

Japan Inc.?

The Economic Miracle

The Japanese economic miracle is the best known and most dramatic of post-second World War economic success stories. Although lacking natural resources and even cultivatable land to support its 117 million people, Japan has become the world's second largest economy. In many sectors – such as electronic goods, cars, and shipbuilding – the leading companies in the world are now Japanese. The standard of living in Japan has risen dramatically, and Japanese wages are now well up the league table of advanced industrialised nations.[1] In short, Japan has become one of the richest countries in the world within a generation, overcoming the disadvantages and problems of losing a world war *en route*.

Many of the reasons for this extraordinary economic success are deep-rooted.[2] Japanese culture has proved to be adaptive yet resilient, accepting many of the ideas and technologies of other countries more readily than most Asian countries yet maintaining norms, many of which have proved to be highly suited to industrial growth. The Japanese have, for example, an extraordinarily high savings propensity, which has enabled them to invest a higher proportion of gross national product (GNP) than their competitors. Japanese culture also instils group solidarity and orderliness, both of which are factors in explaining the almost strike-free record which has advantaged Japan in foreign competition. Nationalism and interlocking social structures have helped to provide Japanese industry with a domestic market protected by custom (as well as, until recently, by formal import restrictions). Japanese workers have a reputation for hard work and reliability which has driven some foreign officials, notably a Commissioner of the EEC, to despair.

(He referred to Japanese workers as 'workaholics'.) Japanese entrepreneurs have displayed an almost extraordinary capacity to overcome the difficulties of distance, language and culture in developing markets overseas. In short, Japan astonished the world.

There were, of course, external factors which helped. The liberal international trade system established after the Second World War provided Japan with access to American and European markets (which it was somewhat slow to reciprocate). Technology could be borrowed from overseas the more easily because Japan was a slow developer and, for the same reason, factories, steel mills and shipyards could be built from scratch in 'green field' sites on optimal lines; they did not just grow in a less than optimal fashion over many decades. Defeat in the Second World War resulted in the imposition on Japan of restraints on defence expenditure which were respected, keeping such expenditures at extraordinarily low levels until American pressure in the 1980s resulted in increased expenditure on 'defence'. Finally, the fact that Japan developed faster than other industrialising countries (rather than simultaneously with them) meant that the strain on the liberal international trade system resulting from Japan's success was not insupportable. Other advanced industrial countries have accepted tremendous damage to their own industries from Japanese competition.

Yet even when all these factors have been taken into account, something is generally thought to be left unexplained. Most observers are agreed that the relationship between business and government in Japan has been crucial in explaining that country's success. How far that relationship can be described as one which turns the whole country into 'Japan Inc.' is one of the questions we must now explore.

Background Influences

It is necessary to begin by discussing general attitudes to business in Japan. The overriding influence on the business–government relationship has been the desire for Japan to catch up.[3] The sudden opening up of Japan to contact with the West by Commodore Perry's ships in 1854 unleashed a struggle within Japan culminating in the victory of those who wished to modernise. Although there was some experimenting with nationalised industries, this process was by and large entrusted to very large-scale private companies, which by the 1930s were known as *zaibatsu* – private business empires. The large enterprise has played a major role in Japanese economic life ever since. Companies provide their workers with a much wider range of benefits (housing and health care, for example) than their counterparts in the West. The Japanese worker who belongs to a union (about 20 per cent of the workforce) is likely to belong to a company union, and the degree of identification by the worker with the company is very high. Large-scale companies provide workers with lifetime security of employment, no doubt partly as a means of fostering this loyalty. The lifetime employment system is made possible by the fact that large-scale enterprises such as Mitsubishi span several industries, and by the absorption of downturns in demand by the significant but often overlooked sector of the economy comprised of small firms, sometimes operated and owned by a single family. It is in fact rare for a large Japanese enterprise to become bankrupt, in spite of the very high level of borrowing by Japanese firms. If a large-scale firm looks to be in real trouble, the banks will appoint new managers, but will generally allow the firm to continue in business.

Class conflict and differences in Japan appear to be very low by Western standards. The low strike record of Japanese workers and the weakness of independent unions have already been referred to. The managers for their part are also careful to minimise potential conflict. Wage differentials between workers and managers are drastically low by Western standards. The Japanese manager also minimises status differences by using the same canteen, starting work at the same time and dressing in the same uniforms as his production workers. In electoral politics, the Japanese Socialist Party receives a small and falling percentage of the vote.[4] Ironically, the Socialists have done particularly badly of late in urban, industrialised areas.

In fact, Japanese politics has been dominated since 1947 by the Liberal Democratic Party.[5] The Party has drawn on a variety of sources for its support, including the declining, inefficient agricultural sector, the middle classes and workers. Though a fragmented party with numerous factions organised around prominent personalities, the Liberal Democrats in turn have been supported financially by industry. The long dominance of Japanese politics by the Liberal Democrats, though they have needed support from independents in recent years, has provided a stable policy background for business. Though the share of the vote taken by the Liberal Democrats has declined, the advantages the electoral system gives them and the disunity of the Opposition parties are likely to ensure their continuance in office indefinitely, adding to their strength some of the very small parties in the Diet (parliament) if necessary.

The stability of Japanese policy is also aided by the strength of the bureaucracy in Japanese government. Before the Second World War the Japanese bureaucracy had to share power with the military and the Emperor's ministers. After the Second World War, during the Allied occupation, the military and ministers lost power while the bureaucracy continued more or less undisturbed, too valuable and necessary an instrument of government to be disrupted by the Allies.[6] Of course, the bureaucracy has a high prestige conferred on it by Japanese culture. To a greater degree even than in Britain, and comparable with France, the civil service has attracted the best and brightest of Japanese graduates. The bonds formed at the top of Japanese universities (notably Tokyo) can be an important source of cohesion in the Japanese bureaucracy. The new civil servant also accepts and, in a manner apparently consistent with many aspects of Japanese life forms a strong attachment to, one of his seniors who provides protection within the civil service and may even assist in such apparently unrelated matters as arranging marriage. The top Japanese civil servants retire relatively young, and may move into either politics or business (two of Japan's recent Prime Ministers are former civil servants). Yet such moves – even into ministerial posts supposedly superior to the civil service – are seen as entailing a decline in status, and are therefore a 'descent from heaven'. The loyalty to the civil service inculcated over the years, and attachments to colleagues remaining within it, are likely to persist even after the civil servant has moved to a new occupation. The former civil servant in business is perhaps more of an opportunity for government – as in France – to influence that business than for business to influence government policy.

The relationship between civil servant and minister is not, therefore, the servant–master relationship that liberal constitutional theory would suggest. On the contrary, it is the civil servant who expects to exert the major influence on policy. The politician exists to represent the ministry in dealings with other departments and to legitimise its policies (if required) in the Diet. The politician, in return, can expect the tolerance of the bureaucracy for political manoeuverings which may add marginally to the costs of departmental policies. The politician is the person who makes the necessary but slightly sordid deals; it is the civil servant who makes the worthwhile policy. The high status the permanent civil servant enjoys compared with the politician again contributes to a stability in policy.

Organisation of Business

Reference has already been made to the importance of the giant enterprises in Japanese business history. Although the importance of the smaller enterprises should not be forgotten, the giant firm still dominates the Japanese economy. This is a fact of some importance. Large organisations are able to represent their own interests directly to government. However, all large enterprises are also members of the *Keidanren*, the very prestigious and influential employers' organisation. The Keidanren is equipped with a large-scale, highly-professional staff which is organised in divisions which parallel those of the Ministry of International Trade and Industry (MITI). This reflects the crucial importance of MITI to Japanese industry about which we shall have more to say. The Keidanren's staff enjoys close personal working relations with the staff of MITI, and are frequently consulted confidentially by them. Indeed, the distinction between the MITI and Keidanren is blurred, and this blurring is encouraged by the recruitment of former MITI staff by the Keidanren. MITI and the Keidanren even exchange junior officials temporarily to ensure that the links between them during their careers will be as smooth as possible. Similar links are forged between the trade associations – such as the Japan Steel League, the Electrical Manufacturing Federation and the Automobile Industry Association – and the relevant parts of MITI.

It should be emphasised that these groups are not only a source of pressure on government; they are also an aid *to* government. The sharing of information between government and industry is obviously of value to government. Beyond this sharing of information, however – which is a common feature of business–government relations in most countries – is the fact that the trade associations and the Keidanren can operate as adjuncts of government. The trade associations, for example, have negotiated directly with their counterparts in countries such as Britain on export limitation agreements to protect the Western country's industry from the full impact of competition with Japan's more efficient industries. Such agreements seem likely to cover more and more industries, illustrating the inter-connection of trade and politics today. The Keidanren itself has made trade agreements with Communist countries, and has organised major projects in Brazil which involve a number of firms.

The Keidanren's links are primarily with the bureaucracy, usually through MITI. The Japanese style of policy-making, which is generally characterised by seeking agreement with interested parties through numerous consultative bodies and agreements, facilitates the Keidanren playing a major role in policy formulation. Figures such as Taizo Ishikaza are prominent in Japanese life to a degree impossible to visualise in the USA or Britain. But the Keidanren also packs a political punch. Funds are collected from the 700 large firms which are members and are given mainly to the Liberal Democratic Party (or rather, as it is an extremely fragmented party, to the different factions within it). The Keidanren's campaign contributions and links with the bureaucracy have been alleged to give large-scale industry (as opposed to small businesses) disproportionate influence. Indeed, small business believes its interests have generally been sacrificed to that of large-scale business. The Keidanren has certainly succeeded in maintaining a pro-business operation in Japanese policy since the Second World War.

Industrial Policy

There is considerable agreement on the importance of the role played by government, particularly the bureaucracy, in Japan's development. It is ironical that so many conservative politicians in Britain and the USA should have failed to see the importance of the role of government in the Japanese success story, a role which they have resisted in their own societies. The exact nature of the role played by MITI as the government agency responsible for fostering industrial development has varied, but has always been concerned with acting as the agent within the Japanese economy which takes a longer perspective than individual firms are likely to.

The Japanese, though very responsive to market pressures and consumer preferences both at home and abroad, have never accepted fully that market pressures alone will bring about satisfactorily necessary industrial change. There must be a disinterested agency, namely MITI, to evaluate trends and their implications for Japanese firms, to seek out opportunities, and draw Japanese firms towards them. But the Japanese are not believers in state control either. There are important examples of industries which have resisted MITI's guidance successfully: the Japanese car industry refused to bow to MITI pressure to consolidate into two firms.

How does MITI make its views effective? As in France, Japan officially has formal state control over private industry. As in France, the reality is more complex. Until the 1970s. MITI did indeed enjoy extensive powers to intervene in the decisions of firms; MITI issued permits which were required to import a wide range of products, and allowed the ministry to control the movement of goods into Japan. Such powers did indeed give MITI strength in structuring Japanese industry; the giant American car manufacturers were by and large prevented from moving into Japan, thus preserving the independent Japanese car industry in the 1940s and 1950s when it could not have resisted a takeover bid from the established American firms. The powers that MITI enjoyed in controlling imports could be used to punish steel firms who did not comply with restructuring plans by cutting their iron ore import allocation. The controls MITI enjoyed over the import of new technology were used to prevent the domination by established American firms of the Japanese electronics and computing market. The difficulties the French experienced with American companies trying to buy the single French computer firm, *Machines Bull*, encouraged the Japanese to take a firm line in protecting their input industry until it could take on – and possibly overcome – the American giant. Even today, MITI controls imports of American manufactured software in order to protect the home industry.

Beyond the formal powers exercised by MITI in the past is the informal power exerted by the Japanese government. As we have noted, Japanese society is highly cohesive and used to government leadership. Japanese firms are also traditionally heavily in debt to banks. The high level of borrowing by Japanese firms is of course one of the reasons for the high level of growth in Japan; it has been said that the Japanese steel firm responds to commercial setbacks by investing more to improve efficiency and product quality, whereas the American firm responds by cutting output and capacity. But the high level of indebtedness has also facilitated the exercise of leadership by MITI. Once MITI has taken a view on future prospects for an industry, the Japanese banking élite is likely to come quickly into line and shape credit policies accordingly. MITI formed the view in the early 1970s, for example, that the textile industry, always labour-intensive, was unsuited to the high-wage economy that Japan was becoming. MITI sought to fulfil its policies by paying grants to textile firms which scrapped textile machinery. The inducements offered by MITI were reinforced, however, by the policies of the banks, which on hearing MITI's dim view of the prospects of the textile industry decided severely to restrict the supply of credit to textile companies (Japanese textile firms have subsequently moved into radically different areas such as pharmaceuticals). MITI's indirect influence is typical of the way in which the Japanese government can influence industry without making orders which are formal, open and therefore able to be questioned by foreigners. The interlocking élites of Japanese government and industry are thus capable of discouraging imports or exports which threaten Japanese trade without issuing orders which might contravene the General Agreement on Tariffs and Trade (GATT).

The image of an omnipotent MITI should be rejected, however. Its concerns have been with the giant firms in Japan, and the important small business sector has – for better or for worse – escaped its attention. The large firms, too, have on occasion defied MITI; we have seen how both the car and steel industries refused to comply with their guidance. Nor should the importance of the entrepreneurial skill of the Japanese businessman be neglected because of a fascination with MITI's role.

The Japanese have also, like the French, lost much of their old ability to control their economy independent of the rest of the world. There has been pressure on the Japanese from their trading partners not only to limit exports, but also to allow in foreign goods and capital. Although the Japanese, like the French, have been adept at using apparently unrelated regulations to bar foreign goods, formal liberalisation of regulations governing the import of goods and capital has taken place. Whether there is a genuine openness to imports is hard for the foreigner to tell because of the opportunities for the veiled, informal but highly effective control described above.

Perhaps more important is the scale of Japanese trade. Though less dependent on foreign trade than Britain, the Japanese clearly depend increasingly on an ability to export in order to finance the imports their society needs, ranging from iron ore to oil. The level of demand for Japanese goods is something obviously beyond the control of the Japanese themselves; both the necessity to trade and the pressures from trading partners have thus made Japan's a less controlled economy than it used to be. MITI still plays an important, vigorous, guiding role, but in a sense it is a victim of its own success. Japan's emergence as a strong, successful nation in international trade has reduced MITI's capacity to *control* the economy. This trend may once more be compared with a similar evolution in French planning.

The success of the Japanese model of government-led growth has naturally attracted the interest of other countries. Three questions have been raised, none of which admit of precise answers. First, to what degree can Japanese growth be explained by the lead given by MITI? Second, why has government leadership of the economy promoted growth instead of fostering inefficiency through the protection of inefficient industries, thus retarding growth? Third, are any of the Japanese institutions transferable to other countries?

We have already mentioned many of the factors involved in answering the first question. The importance of the lead given by MITI has to be weighed against the other possible explanations, such as the high levels of investment, labour productivity and entrepreneurial skills of the Japanese manager. It would be a bold economist, let alone non-economist, who would try to assess precisely the comparative importance of these factors. It is worth noting, however, that behind the Japanese (and French) models of industrial policy is a coherent view of why such policies are necessary. Ordinary businessmen, it is argued, cannot be expected to have the long-term perspective of a government agency. Whereas traditional economics emphasises the speed with which entrepreneurs will adapt to market signals, the Japanese believe that a more structural approach is needed. What is economically rational today – particularly from the perspective of the individual enterprise – is not necessarily rational in the longer term. It may indeed have been rational to allow American car firms to buy a major share in Japanese car firms in the 1950s, or to have bought American computers in the 1970s, but the Japanese economy of the 1980s would have been weaker had such developments been permitted.

The longer-sighted MITI bureaucrats made a better economic decision than the market would have produced. The situation seems to contradict the assumption that government bureaucracies are necessarily slow and unadaptive, prevalent in so many other countries. Yet the system certainly seems to work, perhaps in part because the greatest successes of Japanese industry have come not from inventing totally new products but from making better and cheaper products (such as cars and video cassette recorders) which have been developed elsewhere. Whether the Japanese system can take the lead in developing totally new consumer products remains to be seen. As lower-wage countries (such as South Korea) begin to press the Japanese heavy industries (for example, steel and shipbuilding), such adaptability will prove essential.

Why has government intervention not been led in Japan, as in Britain, into maintaining doomed industries? Such intervention is not unknown in Japan, as her example of agriculture proves. Japan has massively protected its inefficient farm sector in the teeth of American criticism. Yet the pressures to resist industrial change have been contained.

Inevitably, industries do go into irreversible decline in Japan; as the wage rate in Japan increases and labour-intensive industries become more vulnerable to competition from places such as Taiwan or South Korea, such declines may become all the more common. Japan has had to contend since 1973 with the particular problem of paying much higher energy costs when she has no indigenous energy reserves. This again has called into question the viability of formerly strong industries. Eight industries were designated as being in decline in the 1980s – aluminium, cardboard, cotton and wool spinning, electric furnace, steel ferrosilicon, fertilisers, shipbuilding and synthetic fibres. The contrasting fates of these industries illustrates the implausibility of regarding Japan as a homogeneous undifferentiated system.

Declining industries have been assisted by the 1978 Depressed Industries Act. Industries designated under the Act are eligible for government financial assistance and can be exempted from the Anti-Monopoly Law, bequeathed to Japan by the Occupation Administration. The use of the Act has varied from industry to industry. The Act worked most smoothly in the case of shipbuilding. Japan was hit hard by the decline in world demand for ships, particularly super-tankers. The Ministry of Transport arranged a limit on domestic production in line with the trade association (the Shipbuilders Association of Japan). After nineteen companies went bankrupt, the Ministry of Transport succeeded in persuading companies to agree to a 35 per cent cut in capacity. A Shipbuilding Rationalisation Council made up of academics, businessmen, bankers, journalists, and union officials supervised the process, which was, however, planned primarily by the trade association and the ministry. Every effort was made to avoid redundancies, including cutting executives' salaries, dividends, and transferring workers to other jobs, either in a subsidiary or (with the help of the bank) to a job in a supplier's or customer's factory. The banks also helped by rescheduling debt and accepting a moratorium on loan repayments.

The aluminium industry was hit badly by the increase in energy costs. Yet in spite of the obvious danger, the aluminium smelters were unable to arrange a reduction in production. One reason for this is that the aluminium smelters are part of very large companies such as Mitsubishi. Only after several years of heavy losses could MITI arrange a reduction in the scale of the industry, with one entire plant being shipped to South Africa. A similar, and so far even less tractable, problem developed in the electric steel-generating industry. The industry's trade association has proposed that the large firms pay the small firms to go out of business, but the largest firm – the Tokyo Steel Manufacturing Company – refused to comply. It is symptomatic of the changes in Japan that MITI lacked the power to compel obedience, something unthinkable in the 1960s. Indeed, by 1984 the Fair Trade Commission (the anti-monopoly agency) was pressing hard for MITI to lose even more of its powers to suspend or limit competition. Nonetheless, Japan retained (through MITI and its trade associations) a capacity to manage the processes of industrial change in excess of that of Britain or the USA. Increasing competition, particularly from other Asian countries, might make that capacity all the more useful.

The reasons for the ability to contain the inevitable pressures to use government grants to resist change rather than to foster development are fairly apparent. The very success of the Japanese economy reduces pressures; the fear of unemployment is much reduced if an economy is growing. Guarantees of lifetime employment make a similar contribution. Though being shifted to an entirely different part of Japan by a large firm may not be particularly appealing, it is much less alarming than lifetime unemployment. The political system itself, however, also contains pressures. The fact that the Liberal Democrats have been in power continuously since 1948 reduces the importance of inter-party competition. The main motor of the American and British political systems in advantaging geographically-concentrated special interests is reduced in importance by the fact that the Opposition parties, Buddhist or Socialist, have little chance of forming a government. Moreover, the fact that the power of politicians relative to the power of bureaucrats is lower than in Britain or the USA again reduces the power of interests to press for protection. Even if the politicians are inclined to 'give in' to firms or workers seeking government assistance for doomed industries, the civil servants in ministries such as MITI are not. In consequence, the civil servants allow the politicians to make incremental changes in their plans in order to accommodate political deals, but do not facilitate the adoption of policies detrimental to long-term growth or efficiency. The power of the bureaucrat necessarily reduces the power of the politician to bid for votes. It is interesting to note in this context that Japan has also proved particularly resistant to the 'political business cycle'. Whereas there are good grounds to believe that on at least some occasions British and American governments have changed economic policy in order to pick up votes, Japanese fiscal and monetary policies have shown very little variation which can be attributed to electoral pressures. The weakness of party competition and politicians in general would again seem to provide an explanation.

It follows that there are severe limitations to the exportability of the Japanese model. Chalmers Johnson ends his history of MITI by pointing out that there are exceptions even in the USA to the general pattern of government and business having an 'arm's length' relationship if the defence and aircraft industries are obvious cases. One should thus not exaggerate the cultural or institutional barriers to borrowing elements of the Japanese system. However, Johnson also suggests that the Japanese model emerged gradually from the country's past. The Japanese approach to industrialisation in the nineteenth century, the *zaibatsu* in the inter-war period, the wartime administrative structure and the policies followed during the occupation all facilitated the adoption of the system of MITI leadership of private enterprise. Moreover, the balance of power within the political and administrative system which we have emphasised may be also unique to Japan. Certainly, even the supposedly *laissez-faire* Thatcher Government in Britain finds it difficult (if not impossible) to resist political pressures to provide large sums to support such commercially-suspect enterprises as coal, British Leyland and Airbus Industrie. The prospects for a long-term planning system immune to short-term political pressures in England, as in Japan, thus look dim. The crucial importance of geographically-concentrated interests in a competitive party system, coupled with the supremacy of politicians over civil servants, will always incline politicians towards adopting a short-term approach. A similar story can be told of the USA, complicated only by the fragmentation of political power and a lower acceptance of government intervention in the economy than in Britain.

Conclusions

We noted in Chapter 1 that one of the traditional concerns in the study of business and politics was the question of the relative power of business and government. How can Japan be characterised in this respect?

It is clear that many aspects of Japanese life and government are greatly to the advantage of business. The loyalty of Japanese workers to their companies, the weakness of any socialist challenge to the capitalist system and the sheer industriousness of the Japanese might be explained in cultural terms. But many policies of the Japanese government have been more clearly directed to the support of business, particularly large-scale business, than any other country's government. The Japanese government's expenditure on social policies has conversely been lower than in any advanced industrial democracy. The conclusion that business dominates government in Japan is easily supported, too, by reference to the relations between business and government. The political contributions made by business to the Liberal Democrats are open to the criticism that they are bribes; the fact is that Japanese politicians have often been very ready to take actual bribes from corporations. The extremely close links between business and the top bureaucracy also seem to give Japanese business a degree of access to decision-makers unmatched by any other interest in Japan.

Yet a pluralist argument that business dominates government would miss many of the nuances of the relationship. Japanese government has, to an unusual degree for any country, made industrialisation its great central objective. The purpose of the state, as in France, was to secure industrial development – and for many of the same reasons. Both security and economical advance were dependent on economic development. The Japanese state, in its dealings with business, has not been fully controlling, but it has been guiding to a degree not matched even in France. The structural plans of government for industries such as the car industry have been ignored to some degree. But government has usually got its way, and the penalties for firms failing to comply with government plans are nearly always significant. When the Japanese government decided that action was necessary in the 1970s to reduce the severe pollution afflicting Japan, the action taken was firm, resolute and effective. The Japanese rapidly surpassed the USA, let alone Europe, in terms of the severity and vigour of anti-pollution controls, particularly on cars. The speed and effectiveness with which the Japanese government could act in this area suggests that it is not entirely under the thumb of Japanese business. It is rather that business and government share the same objectives.

The closeness of the relationship between business and government is also a conspicuous feature of Japanese politics. In this respect – as in the similarity of objectives between business and government – Japan may be labelled a country which has 'corporatism without labour', whereas properly corporatist countries make major policy – certainly major economic policy – through negotiation or bargaining between government, business and unions. In Japan only business and government are involved. Corporatism has often been seen as a means of reconciling powerful unions with a capitalist system by bringing them into partnership with business and government. In Japan such incorporation of unions has not proved necessary, for unions in Japan (as in France or the USA) have lacked the strength to make their participation in the making of major decisions necessary. At the level of the individual enterprise, the Japanese desire for consensus may well accord a real degree of influence to the leader of even a company union on questions such as whether Nissan should establish a car factory in Britain. However, unions are not involved at the highest levels of policy-making where the drive[7] for consensus bonds only business and government.

The Japanese pattern of business–government partnership has struck many observers as being unique, reflecting the impact on Japanese government and society of a hundred years of trying to catch up and overtake the USA and Europe. Certainly, as we have seen, the leadership role taken by government has been legitimated in part by traditions of authority and governmental practices which stretch back into the nineteenth century and beyond. But is Japan entirely unique? Comparisons with France – at least during the heyday of indicative planning – suggest enough similarities to argue that both are examples of a type: countries with weak unions, a tradition of strong government, and a determination to catch up with more economically-advanced nations. The approach to industrial policy adopted by Japan is not available to other countries with different traditions and political systems, even if they, too, wished to 'catch up'. But there is nothing any more odd about this pattern of business–government relations than about the British or American model. The real difficulties in maintaining the current pattern of government–business relations come from Japan's success. The country's move into international trade where customers are overseas reduces the opportunity for MITI to head Japan's major corporations. Protectionist threats have forced companies such as Nissan to build factories overseas, while the Japanese economy is being opened slowly to foreign goods and capital, both factors reducing the scope for government leadership of the economy. As in the French example, it is possible that government leadership of the economy might be weakened by its own success.

7

The Neo-corporatist Nations

Can Capitalism Survive?

The British often believe they have (and are believed by other people
to have) unusually powerful unions and employers' associations. It is
certainly the case that, by almost any measure, British unions are
stronger than American. Yet British unions in turn can be outmatched
by their counterparts in many European countries, a fact their insular
leaders often overlook. In Norway, Sweden and Austria, for example,
the proportion of the workforce belonging to unions is over 80 per
cent, a far higher proportion than in Britain. Nor is the strength of
working-class movements confined solely to the industrial sector.
In the European countries in which the unions are strongest, not
surprisingly, the Social Democratic Party has also fared well. The
classic example is of course Sweden, where the Social Democrats have
dominated government since the early 1930s, forming the government
continuously from 1936 to 1976. The combination of strong unions
and almost continuous Social Democratic rule might fill the British
or American businessman with despair.

How can capitalism survive in such an environment? In practice,
the neo-corporatist countries such as Austria, Sweden, Norway and,
by some measures, West Germany, have prospered.[1] Austria, for
example, passed from being one of the poorest to one of the richest
West European countries between the end of the Second World War
and the 1970s. Sweden, too, exemplifies a high-income economy,
matching the USA in terms of real income *per capita*. The number
of working days lost per 1000 workers due to strikes has also been
low in the neo-corporatist countries, while levels of productivity

have been very high. In short, in spite of the apparent strength of working-class movements, the neo-corporatist countries have sustained highly successful capitalist economies, providing a congenial setting for business activity: a most successful compromise has been struck between capital and highly-organised labour.

The Concept of Neo-corporatism

Much ink has been spilled in the attempt to define neo-corporatism.[2] Corporatism itself was the belief that people should be represented through functional, occupation-related institutions rather than geographically-defined electoral units. Workers thus would be represented through labour organisations, employers through a business federation, and farmers through a chamber of agriculture. The units of representation would be licensed by the state (and could be controlled by it, therefore), were also charged with carrying out administrative duties on behalf of the state, and were guaranteed a monopoly of the right to represent the relevant part of society. Countries which experimented with this compulsory form of what has been called 'state corporatism' were invariably – and necessarily – ruled by repressive right-wing governments led by Mussolini in Italy, Franco in Spain and Dollfuss in Austria. Not surprisingly, 'corporatist' was not an adjective which states sought to have applied to them after 1945.

Since 1945, however, a number of countries have developed in a manner which might also be labelled corporatist, though the prefix 'neo' or 'liberal'[3] is used to demonstrate that the coercive aspects of state corporatism are absent. The countries are said to be corporatist in that policy is made after close consultation (often amounting to negotiation) with economic interest groups which enjoy a monopoly right to represent farmers, unions and employers, are generally highly centralised, and are entrusted with responsibilities in implementing as well as creating government policies. The countries are 'neo' or 'liberal' corporatist countries because they form governments on the basis of free elections, enjoy democratic rights, and have interest groups which are free (if they choose) to withdraw from their partnership with government. A democratic country can be said *not* to be corporatist if its economic interest groups are fragmented, rarely consulted by top politicians or senior civil servants, and carry out few administrative duties on behalf of the state.

The Function of Compromise

Compromise is a characteristic of the neo-corporatist countries. Indeed, some Austrians have claimed that the *institutions* of compromise in their country are relatively unimportant; it is the spirit which counts. Consultation between the social partners can take the form of a formal meeting, a drink or a meal together, or even a chat in a park. The crucial requirement is solely that consultation in good faith does actually take place. Nonetheless, all the countries covered in this chapter do provide elaborate mechanisms for discussions between the representatives of capital and labour.

Perhaps the best-known example of such institutions of compromise is the Swedish legislative process. The extended process of legislating provides numerous opportunities for interest groups to influence policy. In the early stages of preparing legislation, the government drafts an instruction to a commission to consider the problem at hand within a framework specified by the government. Although such commissions do contain members of the Riksdag (parliament), they have more members who are in effect appointed by the Swedish Employers' Federation or the Federation of Swedish Unions (LO). The commission thus becomes not only an institution for studying problems (like British Royal Commissions) but also a forum for bargaining between government and interests, especially business and labour. The government considers the report of the commission, prepares its final proposals, and then provides interest groups with a further opportunity to influence legislation under the *remiss* procedure in which proposals are forwarded to interest groups for comment before they are sent to the Riksdag. The government's proposals will thus have been discussed extensively in formal meetings with interest groups before the legislative process begins, during which further compromise is common. With some important recent exceptions, a high degree of consensus is reached on legislation, and sharp divisions in the Riksdag are much rarer than in the British parliament. Consultative committees provide similar opportunities for compromise between interests and with government in Norway.[4]

Austria provides an example of formalised meetings between the representatives of employers, unions and the government. The system, known as *Sozialpartnerschaft* (social partnership), or economic partnership (*Wirtschaftspartnerschaft*), grew out of the procedures created to run prices and incomes policy. All Austrians are considered by law members of the appropriate *Kammer* (or Chamber) – the Chamber of Labour, Trade and Industry, or Agriculture. The Chambers are in practice run by the relevant voluntary interest group so that the Chamber of Labour is in practice run by the Austrian Federation of Trade Unions (*Österreicher Gewerkschaftsbund* – OGB). The Chamber of Industry is dominated by the Federation of Industrialists and the Federation of Business, which is the dominant group and is affiliated to the Peoples' Party (OUP) – the unions are of course linked to the Social Democrats who in fact run both the Chamber of Labour and the OGB. The organisations formed the Joint Commission for Prices and Wages during the long 'Grand Coalition' of the OUP and Socialists which governed Austria from 1955–66. The Joint Commission consisted of four government representatives, two from each of the three chambers, and an additional two from the unions (the OGB) as the Chambers of Agriculture and Trade and Industry in practice were allied. The real power in the commission apparently lay with the representatives of the presidents of the Chambers and the OGB to whom all disputes left unresolved by sub-commissions were referred.[5] Sub-commissions were created originally to consider proposals to increase prices and to increase wages, and (after 1963) they were joined by a sub-commission called the Economic and Social Policy Advisory Board with a wider policy approach. The joint participation of the 'social partners' in these sub-commissions is matched in numerous other boards running specific agencies such as the national bank, the ERP (originally the European Recovery Programme) Fund which advances loans to industry at low interest, and on a board which actually determines the level of agricultural subsidies. The Economic and Social Policy Advisory Board provides guidelines for economic policy – for example, determining in the late 1970s that a shift from labour-intensive low-wage industries to higher-wage and higher value-added products was necessary. So numerous and important are the boards on which the Chambers are represented that Austria has been called 'the nation of Chambers'.

The formalisation of contacts between social partners has been more limited in Sweden. Extensive discussions do take place between the Swedish Employers' Federation and the LO on price and pay policies; the government holds itself somewhat in reserve, exerting influence behind the scenes to obtain a desirable outcome. Semi-formal consultations between the government, employers and unions were held, in Erlander's time as Prime Minister from 1946 to 1969, at his country house in Harpsund which then gave its name to the meetings between government and the social partners – known as Harpsund democracy.[6] After criticism of these meetings as excessively secret, they were placed on a more formal basis, being constituted as the Research Council and Planning Board. The Research Council, as the name implies, co-ordinates research on problems of industrial development whilst the Planning Board create long-term economic and investment planning. In the Netherlands, a tripartite council was created by law to serve much the same functions.

Some obvious questions about neo-corporatist systems spring to mind. What are the conditions which have facilitated their emergence? Why are some countries more corporatist than others? And what are the prospects for corporatist systems? Do they have a tendency to collapse or are they relatively stable, enduring systems of government?

Emergence of Corporatist Systems

There is a long tradition of corporatist thought in Catholic countries. Fascists drew on this tradition, but the tradition of corporatist thought was not confined logically or historically to Fascists. Many Catholics, seeking a middle way between socialism and unbridled capitalism, saw advantages in corporatism. Corporatism would give labourers and farmers, as well as entrepreneurs, their place in the social order, a just social order which was neither exploitative nor oppressive. It is not surprising, therefore, that régimes of the Catholic right have done much to lay the groundwork for neo-corporatist systems. The most corporatist of all systems, Austria, was able to build on the corporatist foundations laid by Dollfuss during the First Austrian Republic, and before the *Anschluss* with Germany. Similar tendencies were created in France by the Vichy régime, though the weakness of the post-war French labour movement proved too great a handicap to overcome.

Corporatist systems are at least as abundant outside as inside Catholic Europe, however – Sweden and Norway being the obvious examples. The corporatist countries are more commonly characterised by a tradition of incomes policies centralised bargaining between government, employers and unions about wage (and, less frequently, price) increases. Both Sweden and Austria have generally operated incomes policies in the last 40 years, though incomes policies have been more formalised in Austria than Sweden where government has hovered in the background while the LO and employers reached agreement on the general level of pay increases.

Incomes policies themselves need some explanation: most countries have not pursued them with the consistency of Austria and Sweden. Permanent incomes policies require a number of factors to make them work. First, both unions and employers must be organised in strong, comprehensive labour movements. If labour movements are too weak (in that they organise a comparatively small proportion of the workforce, as in the USA or France), there is not much point in employers bargaining with them through some central, national employers' federation. If power is diffused within the union movement, national bargaining will again be unproductive. In Britain, for example, the TUC is too weak *vis-à-vis* individual unions to sustain a permanent incomes policy, and even the leaders of individual unions enjoy too little power over their members and shop stewards to enforce agreements on them. Much the same can be said of employers' organisations. One of the distinguishing features of Austria's labour movement and employers' organisations is their centralised character. No union would launch a strike without the approval of the OGB, and firms would be liable to legal penalties if they disregarded the Chamber of Trade and Industry in fixing either wages or prices. The question can be pushed back even further, therefore. What facilitates the emergence of centralised unions and employers' organisations?

It is probably the case that strong employers' organisations have been created in response to a strong challenge from unions or a socialist political party. Where unions and socialists have been comparatively weak (as in the USA), employers have been much less cohesive. Strong working-class movements – both unions and socialist parties – have generally emerged in those countries where full citizenship rights (such as the right to vote) have been accorded late so that the struggle to obtain these rights has coincided with the industrial unrest common in the early stages of industrialisation. Sweden is a classic case. Rapid industrialisation in the late nineteenth century was accompanied rather than preceded (as in the USA) by the extension of the right to vote to all (white) men. The extension into the twentieth century of traditional forms of government (the monarchy in Sweden and Britain, the Empire in Austria) increased acceptance of *functional representation* (of farmers, workers and employers, for example) rather than democratic representation: Beer found even in Britain what to him as an American was a surprising emphasis on functional representation.[7]

Incomes policies are found in countries with relatively politically strong labour movements for another obvious reason. Incomes policies are necessary to control inflation only in countries with high rates of employment. If (as in the USA) a pool of marginal labour is always present and comparatively high unemployment is commonly tolerated, the general rate of increase of wages will be moderated by a tendency for supply to outstrip demand. Both Austria and Sweden have needed incomes policies because pressures for full employment have been irresistible. Inflation can be contained in such a situation only through bargaining between employers, unions and government. Naturally unions will wish to discuss in such meetings far more than the degree to which wages should be limited, thereby eating into the powers of both government and management to make autonomous decisions. Discussions broaden from the restraint of incomes into the extent of the welfare state and investment plans.

Tripartite bargaining requires more than suitable institutions, however. It requires an ideological framework congenial to the making of compromises. In Sweden, Austria and the Netherlands, socialists and the unions they dominate have gone far in committing themselves to seeking reforms within the context of a capitalist system. Moreover, special factors have operated in most corporatist countries creating a determination to secure an amicable resolution of differences. In Austria, the fear of a repeat of the disasters of the First Republic in which polarisation led to both dictatorship and *Anschluss* has produced a determination to make the corporatist system work. In Sweden, unions as well as employers are well aware of the need to maintain the competitiveness of Swedish exports if the high standard of living of Sweden is to be maintained. No doubt compromise is also facilitated in the neo-corporatist countries by the fact that they are small (at least in population) and unusually homogeneous (though Sweden has become less so in recent years).

How Enduring are Neo-corporatist Systems?

Neo-corporatist systems have aroused the interest and envy of other states for some years now. Their successes in securing above-average incomes and economic growth with lower than average inflation has fuelled both admiration and envy. It is quite easy, therefore, to find claims that neo-corporatism is a temporary phenomenon, and is already on the decline.

Neo-corporatist systems are open to several lines of attack. The first is that they do not cater for all interests. Groups such as environmentalists and consumer activists will find it difficult to exert influence because interest groups' access to government is blocked by representatives of interests – employers or workers – who are producers. Indeed, any newly-expressed interest or concern may find it difficult to exert influence because the interlocking élites of government, employers, unions and predominantly class-based parties are unreceptive (this may help account for the saying in Austria that issues current in West Germany today will be issues in Austria in three years' time!). Interests which are not easily expressed by unions or employers' organisations thus challenge the legitimacy of a corporatist power system. Environmental and consumer issues have been mentioned as one such challenge; another issue which has been cited in this context is the drift towards the partial or total prohibition of alcohol in Sweden.

A much more serious threat is that the economic interests will cease to be able to compromise on their differences. The most obvious reason for this happening is that economic growth has declined, and perhaps spurred on by the inroads of inflation on real incomes, unions will demand higher wages than employers can afford, or governments tolerate. Such fears proved ill-founded in the 1970s in Austria, and Sweden maintained the corporatist system with somewhat more difficulty. Economic difficulties have, however, reinforced a trend apparent in Europe since before the onset of the current economic crisis – the revival of ideology. The Swedish

Socialists in recent years have moved markedly to the left. Their determination to transfer shares in Swedish companies to union-managed pension funds has led to a breach between the government and employers on a scale unprecedented since the 1930s. In other corporatist countries, economic crisis has moved the centre-right party to the right, seeking to cut government expenditure and taxation to improve the competitiveness of industry. Such moves in the Netherlands have weakened corporatism, taking away some of the welfare state gains bargained for by unions in return for wage restraint. The revival of free-market thought threatens corporatist arrangements as the very legitimacy of representation through social groups (as opposed to representation through legislatures) has been called into question. Fears have moreover been expressed that the institutionalisation of corporatist systems may limit the adaptation of economics to fresh circumstances and technologies, or may handicap them in international markets by creating rigidities inhibiting cuts in wages and social benefits to reduce industrial costs. The least corporatist country – the USA – might thus be better able to adapt to changing circumstances and competition than the corporatist countries.

The Swedish form of neo-corporatism does indeed seem to be in great trouble, and whether it can survive the unrest of the 1980s remains to be seen. Certainly the sight of thousands of managers and executives marching through Stockholm to protest against the government's plans to give shares in companies to union pension funds demonstrated graphically the extent of the decline in the élite consensus and mode of decision-making which had previously characterised the Swedish policy. The long-awaited decline in the stability of neo-corporatist systems should not, however, detract from their real achievements in the 1970s. Schmitter has calculated that the countries commonly ranked as the most corporatist suffered the least citizen unrest and were the least 'fiscally ineffective', i.e. prone to fiscal problems.[8]

Who 'Wins' in Neo-corporatist Systems?

The essence of a neo-corporatist system is that compromises are arrived at between strong centralised organisations representing employers and unions, and the government. It is in the nature of compromise that saying who 'won' or 'lost' is difficult. The balance of power between capital and labour in neo-corporatist countries is further complicated by the fact that neo-corporatist systems typically (and probably necessarily) arise in countries with a strong social democratic tradition, countries in which working-class movements are strong and in which social democratic governments have spent long periods in power. The very high level of welfare expenditure in Sweden, Austria and Norway may be attributed in part to the workings of the neo-corporatist system, and considered the price paid for the willingness of unions to accept wage restraint and changes in working practices. The high level of welfare expenditure is also obviously in part a result of the work of social democratic governments, and is a consequence of their long periods in power in the neo-corporatist countries. Nevertheless, workers in the neo-corporatist countries have typically benefitted from the highest standards of living in the world, the most generous welfare and retirement provisions, and the lowest unemployment levels. No doubt some would consider that unions or social democratic parties in the neo-corporatist countries have shown insufficient militancy or zeal for socialism. The contrast between the economic records of Austria and Britain may suggest why militancy or socialist zeal have been lacking, and what the compensations have been.

What of life for employers under neo-corporatism? Obviously the high levels of taxation have not appealed particularly to high-paid executives, and the neo-corporatist countries have comprehensive regulations covering the environment, workplace safety and health, and consumer protection. Yet the governments of neo-corporatist countries have shown a lively awareness of the need to maintain the competitiveness of their industries; as noted above, the Swedish Socialists did not nationalise industries in part because they wished to preserve their industries' freedom of action in international markets. It was the Conservative Government elected in 1976 which broke the Swedish tradition of not interfering with market mechanisms by subsidising individual companies. When the Socialists returned to power, they reduced such subsidies and insisted that firms be commercially viable without government help. Kelman[9] has also shown that regulations in Sweden are enforced less dogmatically, less legalistically and more realistically than in less corporatist states such as the USA. Swedish inspectors are more likely than American to see it as their duty to persuade or cajole rather than coerce employers into action. The 'business climate' of the neo-corporatist states is thus less difficult than might be supposed. Moreover, many of the norms common in the neo-corporatist countries – norms of orderliness, of seeking compromise, and perhaps even a certain lack of individual assertiveness – help to produce disciplined, hard-working labour forces. The neo-corporatist institutions geared towards the production of compromise have grown out of, rather than been imposed upon, social norms and patterns which are themselves productive of good industrial relations.

Conclusions

Fashions change in political science. In the 1970s the neo-corporatist nations were much admired as better able to cope with oil shocks and contain inflation than less corporatist nations. In the mid-1980s the least corporatist nation (the USA) is admired for its ability to adapt to new circumstances and technologies. The relative strengths and weaknesses of the USA and the less corporatist countries may be reassessed if the USA proves unable to resolve its government or trade deficits.

Neo-corporatism is not, however an option available to be taken or rejected at will. On the contrary, neo-corporatism (like the government–business partnership in Japan) is the product of special circumstances which include political culture, government and interest-group culture. There would be no point in an American president resolving to have a more corporatist system: the circumstances are not ripe. Neither would it be possible for a Swedish or an Austrian Prime Minister to resolve not to have a neo-corporatist system. Neo-corporatism is *the* (or at least *a*) method of reconciling capitalism with strong unions and socialism. To deny the Swedish or Austrian unions a role in policy-making would be to invite severe trouble. The neo-corporatist systems, however uncertain their futures, have provided their inhabitants with 30 years of high employment, low inflation and considerable economic growth. It is a record which Britons might envy, though not a practice it might readily replicate.

8

The Multinationals – Companies without Governments?

The Transnational Company

One of the more dramatic developments of this century has been the expansion of companies across national boundaries. Today's motorist can drive in Europe or the USA without abandoning his or her favourite brand of petrol; the company that has franchised and supplied the petrol station might well be one of the 'Seven Sisters' of the oil industry which has extracted the petroleum from the ground in Saudi Arabia, the north slope of Alaska, or the North Sea, has transported it to a refinery it owns and operates in a consumer country and has organised its sale to the ordinary motorist. The car which the motorist drives may well be a car produced by a company which is itself manufactured in Europe but whose headquarters is in the USA. Numerous of our motorist's other needs may be supplied by similarly 'crossnational' companies. The soap in which the motorist washed before leaving the house, the word processor which the motorist uses at work, and the films watched for entertainment in the evening may all be manufactured by companies whose headquarters are in one country but which have manufacturing capacity in others.

It is not surprising, therefore, that the multinationals, as they are called, are seen as one of the major features of the current world economy. Multinationals, precisely because of their importance in daily life and obvious size, can also seem threatening embody to the highest possible degree the privileged position of business that Lindblom described. In an extreme case, a multinational may actually decide that the policies of a country, or the strength of its unions, are such that the multinational will pull out, closing or selling its plants. More likely is the possibility that a multinational will more gradually reposition itself, concentrating investment in countries which provide the most congenial policies, lowest wages or highest productivity. The Ford Motor Company, for example, has manufacturing capacity in the USA, Canada, Britain, Belgium, West Germany and Spain, amongst other countries. Such a spread of manufacturing capacity enables the multinational to respond to purely economic or commercial considerations, or to exert very obvious and direct pressure on a host government for changes in policy to its advantage. A somewhat crude example involved the Chrysler Corporation, which in addition to the subsidies it obtained from the US government received major payments from the British government in return for keeping open the company's plants in Britain. The British government, fearing that closure of the plants would add to rising unemployment, felt that it had no option but to pay up. Ironically, a few years later the Chrysler Corporation sold its plants in Britain to the French company, Peugeot. Less crude (and perhaps less precise) pressures on politicians help to account for decisions such as the rapid shelving of proposals during the 1974–9 Labour Government for a measure of worker participation lest Britain be thought an even less desirable place to invest than it was already.

The ability of multinationals to relocate should not be exaggerated. It so happens that the majority of the known oil reserves in the world are in the Middle East and the Middle East's reserves are unusually easy and cheap to extract. Although Alaska and the North Sea may be more attractive politically, they are not as easy environments in which to operate in terms of the engineering required. The copper reserves of Chile operated by Kennecott cannot be moved outside the country; the diamond or gold mines of South Africa have no counterparts which can be developed as easily outside the Soviet Union. Multinationals, particularly in the extractive industries, must often grin and bear conditions which they dislike because, until alternatives are developed, no substitutes are available. The oil industry is perhaps the most interesting to watch in this respect. For obvious reasons – including the tendency of more radical Arab governments to impose more onerous conditions and taxes on multinationals – the oil companies have been prepared to develop other sources of supply. Their ability to move towards production in politically safer environments is limited by the differential costs of production. It has been argued, however, that the oil companies' greatest problems arise when they wish to operate in politically unstable regions where no régime lasts long enough for them to make a lasting deal. Such problems may have prevented serious exploration of possible oil reserves in Africa, and suggests that one of the greatest gains for multinationals from the colonial era may have been the stability of colonial régimes.

The abilities to move funds and redirect investment are not the only powers enjoyed by multinationals. One of the crucial resources enjoyed by multinationals is *knowledge*. The multinational companies often do not bring the majority of the capital needed to a branch they create in a country; the majority of funds may well be raised locally. The major contribution of the multinational to the local enterprise may be knowledge, knowledge that may range from the secret formula for making Coca Cola to life-saving drugs. The oil companies again provide an example. The 'Seven Sisters', the giant firms that dominate the oil industry, have been able to survive in the more radical countries because they have more knowledge, or skills, at their disposal in oil extraction than could be readily available to the governments themselves. It has been quite common for oil companies to see their assets nationalised only to be immediately re-employed by the nationalising government as its agent, receiving a commission on the oil extracted and sold instead of a profit. Oil companies are also more experienced and better placed to organise the raising of investment funds than are many governments, which have in some cases vowed to drive them out of their countries. When exploration and development of the British North Sea oil fields began, the British government of the day, while giving some of the reserves to a government-owned corporation, was delighted by the positive impact on the British balance of payments of the movement into Britain by the multinational oil companies of funds to finance development. This ability to raise finances may again provide a powerful inducement for governments to make a deal with a multinational they publicly attack. Governments as far apart as Norway and Bahrain have for such reasons entrusted most of the development of their reserves to multinationals.

The powers of the multinationals which we have described so far are considerable, and yet might be said to be the inevitable consequence of the existence of multinational firms. The executives of multinational companies could not ignore factors such as government policies in making investment decisions without what might be seen as quite scandalous disregard for the interests of their shareholders. More controversial, however, is the question of the extent to which multinationals engage in what might be widely-regarded as illicit interference in the politics of the countries in which they operate. Obviously no one could object to a multinational joining the trade associations and the employers' organisation of a country in which it operates. There is no reason why the Ford Motor Company in Britain should be barred from joining the CBI. Yet there are a number of disturbing examples, from Europe as well as Africa and Asia, of multinationals exerting political pressure which crosses the boundaries of acceptability. Lockheed paid bribes around the world and, even worse, multinationals operating in Chile used a wide variety of weapons to attack the constitutionally elected, if minority, government of Salvador Allende. Money was given to Opposition parties, an economic blockade of Chile was organised, and multinationals urged both domestic dissidents and the government of the USA to assassinate or overthrow Allende.[1]

The activities of multinationals in Chile remind us of a further point. We noted earlier that the term 'multinational' could be misleading because most firms are firmly based in one country. The government of that parent country will be asked to assist in cases in which the interests of the multinational are attacked. The American multinationals operating in Chile soon asked the American government to unleash the Central Intelligence Agency (CIA) against the Allende government once that government's threat to expropriate their assets, in return for what they regarded as inadequate compensation, became clear. The American government tightened the screws on Chile by using its influence in international financial institutions to block loans; the CIA, which had long been the primary source of funds for the pro-business parties in Chile, encouraged plots against the government – on one occasion supplying revolvers for an abortive assassination attempt on General Schneider, the Chief of Staff, whose attachment to constitutional government was a major barrier to the military coup which ultimately occurred.[2]

The destruction of constitutional government in Chile, brought about by internal as well as external forces, is a particularly painful example of intervention. It is not, unfortunately, unique. The government of Guatemala was also overthrown with considerable American help, in part because it was a threat to the interests of United Fruit which has large investments there. One is reminded of the comment of US Marine General Smedley D. Butler in 1931 as he looked back on his career:

> I helped make Mexico safe for American oil interests in 1914. I helped make Haiti and Cuba a decent place for the National City Bank boys to collect revenues in. I helped purify Nicaragua for the International banking house of Brown Brothers...I made Honduras 'right' for American fruit companies. Looking back on it, I might have given Al Capone a few hints.[3]

It is a great advantage for multinationals that, though they may invoke the assistance of the government of the parent country, they may also keep their distance from it. Firms which are thought to be domestically owned stir up less nationalist resentment. Really powerful firms such as the oil companies may prefer to rely upon their technical and financial power rather than the military or domestic pressure of 'their' government in dealings with countries in which they wish to operate. It is certainly the case that multinationals are often devoid of feelings of loyalty to the home country. When British Prime Minister Edward Heath told the head of British Petroleum (BP) during the first oil crisis (1973) that he was counting on BP to make supplying Britain its first priority, he was told to think again. Both BP and Shell, in spite of their British connections, were active in supplying the rebel régime in what was then Rhodesia with oil, thus undermining the sanctions which British government were trying to impose upon Rhodesia. This is given added irony by the fact that BP was a company in which the government had a major – almost a majority – shareholding.

Multinationals and the Third World

Particular concern has been expressed about the relationship between multinationals and Third World countries. The term 'Third World' is, of course, ambiguous and broad. Countries such as Argentina certainly resent being bracketed with Chad, and whether there are worthwhile analogies to be drawn between Latin American and African countries may indeed be doubted. Yet a number of common problems do arise for the less-developed countries in dealing with multinationals which exacerbate the criticisms of multinationals which we have encountered. Less-developed countries are likely to be particularly short of capital, and by definition desperately in need of generating employment and economic growth. Such countries are therefore even less able to bargain successfully with multinationals than are developed countries. Developing countries are also less able to use the normal government weapons to restrain their power. Few developing countries have a civil service of sufficient size and skill to monitor the activities of multinationals, or to impose the environmental or safety standards which would be regarded as essential in developed countries. The dreadful disaster in Bhopal, India, following the escape of poisonous gas from a Union Carbide Factory in the town demonstrated vividly the tolerance of lower safety standards in the Third World. Local cultures in many less-developed countries and poor pay for officials or lack of accountability for leaders combine to make bribery endemic, a practice which multinationals can follow without financial embarrassment.

The host government may thus be totally incapable or unwilling to control the activities of multinationals. Even an honest government in a less-developed country may suffer from a chronic inability to collect information, except such information as the multinational chooses to give it. Efforts to tax multinationals have been impeded by their ability to transfer goods at unrealistic prices between branches in different countries so as to minimise tax – a practice that the civil service of a very advanced country would have difficulty checking. An extremely high 'price' may be paid by a subsidiary to a parent company for machinery or a process supplied by it, thus reducing the taxable profits of the subsidiary. Alternatively, goods from the subsidiary may be sold at an inflated price to the parent company in order to minimise its taxable earnings. Both strategies may be combined by using as an intermediary a third branch of the company located in a country such as Panama with low corporate taxation, the subsidiary buying and selling from other branches of the multinational at artificial prices. Such manipulations, beyond the capacity of most Third World civil services to check, may make meaningless the profit figures declared by a multinational.

A further criticism of multinationals, all the more important for involving no allegation of conspiracy or malevolence, is that they distort the development of Third World countries. Such criticisms focus on allegations that multinationals deploy inappropriate technology in the Third World. Third World countries generally have a chronic over-supply of labour. If multinationals deploy technologies in the Third World which are capital-intensive but which use little labour, they are bringing to the Third World country a technology which is inappropriate to its needs. Developing a new, more labour-intensive technology may be uncongenial or unprofitable for the multinational; moreover, the multinational's workers, and particularly its managers, may come to be not only a commercial but a social intrusion into the life of the country. The Western-trained and Western-oriented élite fostered by the multinational will look to the advanced countries when they are looking for a home for their savings, for luxury goods, or for a university to which to send their children. All of these practices may have a most deleterious effect on the usually precarious balance of payments of the developing country, and contribute to its usual chronic shortage of foreign exchange. Multinationals, in short, may act as agents to spread 'dependency' upon developed countries.

Finally, multinationals are criticised for remitting profits from developing countries to the home country. Countries already short of capital must thus endure a further flow back to the developed world. Ironically, multinationals will be criticised in the developed world for exporting capital and jobs to the Third World, slowing growth and reducing the number of jobs in the home country. Thus no one may be satisfied.

The Case for Multinationals

So far we have considered only the case for the prosecution against multinationals. Naturally, the multinationals think that much can be said on their behalf.

As their critics have contended, multinationals can be instruments of technological diffusion. Certainly such technological diffusion may be conducted in a manner not conducive to the interests of the recipient country, but it is easy to make a contrary argument. It is not good economic sense for a multinational to substitute capital for labour if suitable labour is available. Company profits, as well as the recipient country, would suffer. Nor is it obvious that critics of the multinationals would be satisfied if they restricted the Third World to simple technologies. It is noticeable that India, to the despair of many international advisory bodies, has been determined to conduct advanced research on atomic power and space programmes rather than concentrating exclusively on schemes which would have a high demand for manpower. Moreover, it is by no means proven that multinationals do impose overly advanced technologies on Third World countries; practice almost certainly varies considerably from firm to firm. Theorising on the practices and consequences of multinationals runs far ahead of empirical research.

It might also be noted that, contrary to the arguments of the 'dependency' theorists, multinationals have not been a complete barrier to development in the past. Much of Sweden's economic development was carried out earlier this century by multinationals; Canada combines a high standard of living with extensive domination of its economy by American firms, a domination which does indeed cause problems but which has not been crippling. One might doubt, too, whether the Latin American students and academics who flock to London or Paris are there because of the activities of a British or French multinational.

Both critics and friends of multinationals have been forced to concede in recent years that the extent of the impact of multinationals on capital movements has been exaggerated. Multinationals have often argued that they fulfil a useful social purpose by distributing capital to the Third World. In practice, it seems that multinationals bring little capital into countries; most subsidiaries of multinationals are apparently created by organising capital, much of it local, rather than by bringing in *tranche* of funds from the parent company. Whether the repatriation of profits made with these funds is justified depends on one's point of view. Such profits can be termed surplus value in Marxist terminology, or rewards for entrepreneurship in more conventional economics.

Perhaps the most useful contribution made by multinationals is the one which could not be fulfilled by any democratically-elected government and is often wildly unpopular in the parent country.

This is the function of transferring to developing countries the production of goods which require large quantities of low-cost labour. Low-cost labour is one commodity which less-developed countries possess in abundance. If developing countries are ever to progress economically, they must be allowed to capitalise on this 'natural advantage' by making textiles or assembling electrical equipment for sale in the more prosperous countries. Such an 'export' of jobs would not be tolerated willingly by elected governments, but can be arranged – barring effective protectionist measures – by multinationals. In the last analysis it may be, too, that the prospects for a developing country turn more on whether its local entrepreneurs and middle class have the character of the Korean, Taiwanese and Singapore, or whether they have the aversion to trade and commerce found in many Latin American countries.

It may also be that the significance of multinationals for the Third World has been exaggerated. Multinationals are largely a phenomenon of the developed world. In the years since the Second World War Europe, not the Third World continent, has been the favourite investment area for American multinationals, and European firms such as Volkswagen have been expanding into the USA. The activities of multinationals do indeed pose problems for the governments of developed countries, but those problems are more manageable for them than for their Third World hosts. Developed countries have stronger governments, better equipped with skilled bureaucracies than are Third World countries. Moreover, the exchange of multinationals which now characterises the relations between most of the developed world is less likely to result in exploitation than when a country is only a host for, not a source of, multinationals.

Controlling the Multinationals

It remains the case that multinationals are not susceptible to control by any one national government. Problems of control which overwhelm the governments of less-developed nations are not fully solved by developed countries. A country which sets its face against multinationals (as France did with American car firms in the 1960s) risks losing them to a neighbour, such as Belgium, who exports their products to the resistant country. Japan excluded American car firms while developing its own car industry in the 1950s, but whether any country could follow suit in the liberalised trade atmosphere of the 1980s may be doubted. Even Japan is under heavy pressure to allow in not only foreign goods but also foreign capital as it liberalises its restrictions.

Organisations linking nations offer some prospect of increasing controls over the multinational. The EEC, the most developed of such multinational government organisations, has started to create regulations on such topics as health and safety at work which in theory will be enforced in all member nations. Thus the multinational loses some ability to offer new investment to the nation with the laxest standards. But regulations are not enforced equally stringently in practice, e.g. Italian inspectors are not as thorough as Danish. Even within the more tightly-integrated economy of the USA, federalism allows individual states to bid for new factories from corporations by varying taxation and regulation, and Europe is far less integrated than the USA.

It might be advisable for host countries to try to weaken the hold of any one multinational by inviting in more, particularly if they are of a different national origin. Multinationals, particularly in the Third World, tend to be geographically concentrated in terms of their national origin. American multinationals account for over three-quarters of foreign holdings in Latin America, while British multinationals are more likely to operate in Africa. It may well be wise for host countries to create the possibility of dividing and ruling by inviting in multinationals of a different nationality than those already present. Such diversification may also be advisable economically. Modelski points out that whatever their political strength, multinationals are not invulnerable commercially. On the contrary, multinationals are subject to the pressures of competition, too. Twenty-seven of the firms which were amongst the top 50 largest firms in the world in 1955 were not in those ranks in 1975; several had disappeared completely and others had been taken over by larger firms. Modelski concludes that 'the significant fact seems to be the relative transience of world status', a fact of some relevance not only to the multinationals but to the countries whose economies are entrusted to them.[4]

Conclusions

It would be idle to pretend that diversification or further development of regional blocks such as the EEC will solve all the problems of the multinationals' influence in world affairs. The threat to political control and autonomy becomes apparent when posed by the simple fact that the ten largest multinationals have turnovers in excess of the total GNP's of 80 nations. But multinationals are not in practice regarded as all bad; both the British Government and Labour MPs from areas where the factory might be located begged Nissan Motors of Japan to locate in Britain, strengthening its development into being a multinational. Indeed, it might well be that protectionist pressures will encourage more and more firms to become multinationals, setting up manufacturing plants inside trading blocks, such as the EEC, which might erect barriers against them. If the multinational is to become more and more common, an increase in empirical research, perhaps at the expense of theorising, would be welcome. As Vernon argues, [5] generalisations about multinationals are dangerous. Different firms, different countries and even different government agencies create different situations. At the very moment that the CIA was operating on behalf of United Fruit in Guatemala, the Justice Department's Antitrust Division was trying to break up the company! Research on individual companies will not be easy; they are more secretive than governments. Yet the flow of accusation and counter-accusation discussed above can be avoided only by theoretically conscious research.[6]

9

Conclusions

The Continuum of Business–Government Relations

If any one theme has emerged from the previous eight chapters it is that there is no single pattern to the relationship between business and politics in the countries we have surveyed. The differences take a variety of forms. In particular, the degree to which business has organised into trade associations representing employers in a particular industry, and the degree to which employers in different industries have joined together to protect their collective interests, differ considerably from country to country. The countries covered in this book can be arranged on a continuum in this respect. At one extreme, trade associations in the USA have in the recent past enjoyed little prestige, while the competition for the role of being the peak association speaking authoritatively for American business to Congress and the Executive has been intense; the NAM, the Chamber of Commerce and the Business Roundtable have all lodged claims to the role. In contrast in Japan, at the other end of the continuum, the Keidanren has a clear role as the voice of Japanese business, speaking authoritatively to Japanese government on behalf of all major Japanese firms and industries. In terms of the cohesiveness of business – as we may call this factor – the continuum may run from a low point of business cohesiveness in the USA, to a higher degree of organisation in Britain, France, Germany, through the neo-corporatist countries such as Sweden or Austria, finally to reach, at the other end of the continuum, Japan.

Government and Business Organisation

The relationship between government and business organisations in countries in which business is highly organised into trade and peak associations is not to be understood as necessarily (or even primarily) adversarial. It has been traditional in both Britain and the USA to think of business organisations being outside government, acting, in the usual phrase, as 'pressure groups'. This very phrase suggests a distance and a separation of function between business organisations and government which would not make sense in many countries. Business and trade associations have fulfilled a variety of functions, not against but for government. These functions have included the management of wage/price policy in Sweden and Austria and the conduct of trade negotiations in Japan, where the Keidanren has made binding agreements with its counterparts abroad on the restraint of Japanese exports. Examples of trade associations fulfilling functions for government (as opposed to exerting pressure on it) can be found in Britain, too, and even in the USA. Yet, perhaps because research has not fully demonstrated the extent to which business organisations do indeed act on behalf of government in Britain and the USA, and also partly because government actually makes less use of such business organisations, it remains more common to think of business organisations in those two countries as outside pressure groups than as groups incorporated into the framework of government. This tendency is strongest in the USA.

Electoral Politics

It is also clear that there is substantial variation in the degree and manner in which business engages and participates in electoral politics. In every country which we have surveyed there is no doubt that there is one party much closer to business than others. Substantial variation exists, however, in the stress that business puts on supporting its friends electorally (as opposed to interest-group activities), and the manner in which this support is expressed. In the USA business has put as much stress in recent years on developing its capacity to help friendly politicians through campaign contributions from Political Action Committees (PACs) as it has placed on lobbying. In Sweden, in contrast, the links which undoubtedly exist between business and the 'bourgeois' parties are played down lest they interfere with the role of the Swedish Employers' Federation as a pressure group. On the other hand, American laws (and, since the Watergate affair, American practice) have raised a stronger barrier between the normal funds of corporations and their political contributions than would be the case in Britain or in West Germany. The British practice of allowing corporations to spend what they wish from their normal operating funds to aid the party of their choice is no longer permitted in the USA.

It is also the case that the countries we have surveyed differ in terms of the degree to which the pro-business party is one shared by other interests, too. It has been the case in Britain in the past, and in Japan today, that the pro-business party also stands for other interests. It is ironic, given the practice of thinking of the USA as a country whose politics are controlled by business, that the link between the Republican Party and business is less organic than the link between Japanese business and the Liberals or British business and the Conservative Party. Not all business interests have identified with the Republican Party in the past (Texas oil was quite happy with the Southern Democrats), and although nowadays the Republican Party has more solid business support, that support is not unanimous. Moreover, the Republicans have courted such diverse interests as the corrupt but militant Teamsters Union, and the religious fundamentalists of the Moral Majority. Indeed, the executives of the largest corporations would be treated with more suspicion than respect by many of the right-wing zealots now so strong in the Republican Party. It is the more *laissez-faire*, 'Sun-belt' industries which now dominate the Republican Party, enhancing the Chamber of Commerce's influence but weakening that of the Business Roundtable, which speaks for the larger, more established company. Few such complexities surface in the relationship between the business communities and 'their' parties in Austria or Sweden.

The Challenge to Business

How might these variations in the patterns of business involvement in government and politics be explained? A number of different factors may be seen as crucial. First, and perhaps most important, is the degree to which business executives have perceived that they are faced with a major *challenge*. Business has not gone unquestioned or unchallenged in any country, but the degree to which it has been confronted with a strong, permanent opposition has differed considerably. The strongest and most permanent challenges to business came traditionally from working-class movements, unions and Socialist parties. It is precisely in those countries in which employers have encountered a significant threat from an organised working class – countries such as Britain, Sweden, Norway, Austria and Germany – that employers, too, have created strong organisations. The USA, the country in which the challenge to capitalism has been the weakest, is also the country in which employers' organisations have been the most fragmented. In the USA in recent years a significant challenge to business practices was mounted by the public interest groups and, interestingly (as we should have predicted), this was followed by a sharp increase in the level and even cohesiveness of business participation in politics. Unfortunately, that challenge has not been sufficiently strong or persistent to permit an assessment of the full potential of American employers to organise, and as the challenge of the consumer and environmental movements was contained, so the fragmentary tendencies of American business groups reappeared. On the other hand, it would not be entirely plausible to say that the degree of challenge to employers is the only factor explaining their readiness to organise. Japan's socialists were stronger in the past than they are now, but neither they nor the unions have ever caused Japan's employers too much concern.

It is, of course, necessary to remember that it is the *past* degree of challenge which has been suggested as an explanation of the extent to which business is organised. No one would suggest that employers in Austria, West Germany or Sweden today should lie awake worrying about the challenge to capitalism from their countries' unions or Social Democrats. The German or Austrian unions were not always so reformist, however, and were certainly sufficiently radical and militant to provide an impetus to employers to organise. Of course, once organisations have been created they may have a tendency to persist. Yesterday's employers' organisation, formed to combat the Red menace, may as easily become a technocratic organisation to work in partnership with government and unions. It is the past, not the current character, of the challenge to business which explains the degree of its current organisation.

Political Culture

A second factor which has played a vital role in shaping the political role and involvement of business has been the *political culture* of the country in which it has been operating.

One aspect of the political culture which has an impact on the nature of business organisation may be linked to our argument above – in countries such as the USA in which the political culture has been highly favourable to business, the incentive to organise for the protection of business's collective interests has been less than in political cultures more likely to sustain a challenge to business. Although too much stress on the 'liberal tradition' of the USA has faced challenges on specific issues from populists, progressives, environmentalists, consumer groups and even (in the New Deal era) advocates of the government ownership of electric power generation, the unpopularity of socialism has always been an important factor.

Political culture exerts another influence, however. The degree to which what Beer called in the British context 'functional representation'[1] is accepted varies from country to country. The extreme cases of acceptance of functional representation are of course the neo-corporatist countries. It is widely accepted in Austria that the leaders of the unions and employers' organisations should have more opportunity to influence the conduct of economic policy than the vast majority of elected politicians. Such a view would not be entirely accepted in Britain itself, in spite of the fact that, as Beer noted, functional representation was an important component in the British political system and culture. Many Britons were deeply concerned when commentators in the 1970s told them that government was paying more attention to the views of major economic interest groups than to the views of MPs. In Norway or Austria such concerns would have been seen as irrational; partnership between government and the major economic groups is merely a fact of life, a process that enables better policy to be made and ensures social harmony. Representation through major economic groups was an effective and legitimate means for the representation of the individual citizen.

The British are in this, as in so much else, a halfway house between the USA and Europe. If the British are uneasy and uncertain about functional representation, Americans are unambiguously hostile. The very idea that the major economic interests could exert great influence on policy behind closed doors – greater influence than a member of Congress – would be cause for deep concern. 'Big unions' and 'big business' are targets of popular criticism, not bases of representation.

It would be fascinating but difficult to explain the origins of these political cultures. As we have noted, the tradition of functional representation in Germany and Japan stretches far back into the history of the *Kammern* (medieval chambers of commerce). The question of whether industrialisation was carried out independently of government or (as in Japan and Germany) in partnership with it is also relevant. The fact that the USA was, as a political system, a child of the Enlightenment born after the passing of the medieval tradition and was industrialised by entrepreneurs acting independently of the government, helps to explain the extreme weakness of functional representation in the American political culture. The British political culture may well have been influenced in part by the long continuity of British society with its medieval legacies, and in part by the fact that Britain was the exemplar of industrialisation through the private sector. In Japan, the legacies of feudalism and of government-led industrialisation combined to legitimise the extremely close partnership between business and government, where the business–government distinction all but disappears.

Political Structure

The political structure of a country also exerts a powerful influence on the form of business–political involvement; countries which have strong, centralised governments are more likely to have strong, centralised interest groups. This is in part because interest groups are less likely to be able to develop a 'clientelistic' relationship with the part of government which is of the most concern to them, and so must organise to exert influence on the government as a whole. It is also in part because governments which are sufficiently strong to limit access will encourage a centralisation of interest groups in order to avoid the embarrassment of having to choose between the claims of contending groups within the same sector. From the viewpoint of a politician – particularly a politician who has no particularly clear or strong views on a subject – it is far better to have conflicts of interest or viewpoint 'brokered out' within the interest group than for the politician to have to decide which group (or sub-group) to support.

It is noticeable that the British government, one of the most cohesive we have encountered, uses its ability to control the access of interest groups to decision-makers at a stage when the government is sufficiently undecided to make consultation potentially effective, not to ban interest groups entirely but to limit access to a group able to speak for the entire sector. Such 'insider groups' gain the best possible opportunity to influence policy, though in return for this insider status they are expected to make moderate demands, respect confidences and not campaign too 'politically' against the government. Most important for our purposes is that the government uses this ability to restrict access to build up the most comprehensive interest groups by refusing to deal seriously with rivals. British governments long refused to deal with the Farmers' Union of Wales in order to bolster the authority of the NFU; within the industrial sector, the CBI was brought into existence at the behest of government, which was anxious to have a comprehensive, authoritative body to deal with in its attempts at planning in the 1960s. The CBI's authority has since been maintained (in spite of occasional resignations by firms which think it too moderate) because the government consults closely with the CBI, and invites it to appoint on behalf of industry representatives to run bodies such as the Health and Safety Commission and Manpower Services Commission. Centralised government thus sustains centralised interest groups.

The nature of the party system is another influence on the structure of business participation in politics. In the tightly-structured party systems of Britain or West Germany, business groups can do little other than support the more pro-business party financially. More open or permeable systems present additional opportunities and challenges. The highly factious nature of the Japanese Liberal Party allows – or perhaps even requires – the business groups of Japan to contribute not only to the party itself but to the different factions within it.

In the USA, the high cost of campaigning and the highly-permeable, ill-disciplined nature of the political parties allows business to pick candidates (usually – but not always – Republicans) to fund and support through the contributions of the PACs. Although the increasing role of PACs in American politics has aroused alarm, in some ways the situation is more regulated now than it was in the comparatively recent past. In the aftermath of Watergate, the revelations of the large and wholly illegal contributions to campaigns by many of America's best-known companies led to limits being imposed on the amount that PACs could contribute ($5000 per candidate per election) and ended the extensive practice of corporate executives making large-scale, secret contributions on behalf of their employers; individuals were allowed to contribute only $1000 per candidate per election, and strictly on their own behalf. The high cost of campaigning and the availability of funds from PACs may still foster an unhealthy dependence of politicians upon interest groups, but at least it is now a more open dependence in which 'who gave what to whom' can be discovered from the records of the Federal Elections Commission.

Whether it is really conducive to the maximum influence of business to be driven into such open involvement in political finance is uncertain. The resources provided by business PACs to their favoured candidates are sufficiently lavish to give them a real advantage in campaigning; business-associated PACs and their allies contribute considerably more to political campaigns than the next largest spenders (labour unions) by a margin of about three to two. Yet even in the USA (or at least in parts of the USA), over-dependence on business can be a real disadvantage for a candidate, and in countries such as Britain the more veiled, less-publicised contributions of companies to the more pro-business party is a much less risky method of financing friends.

A final factor influencing the structure of business involvement in politics is the question of whether the political system is unitary or federal. Federal systems encourage federal pressure groups, including federal employers' organisations. In both the USA and West Germany, the important powers enjoyed by states and the *Länder* have ensured that important functions are fulfilled by state branches of employers' groups. In contrast, the centralised countries such as France and Great Britain have equally centralised employers' associations whose regional structures are weak. Federal systems probably enhance the power of business in several respects. State governments are seen as more open to business influence in the USA than is the federal government, partly because pressure groups in general are thought to be more powerful in state than in federal politics. Most important of all is the fact that (in Lindblom's language) the privileged position of business is bound to be greater when the power and roles of government are decentralised to a significant number of governments. Business can play one state government against another, threatening to move to another state if the 'business climate' is not improved satisfactorily. Readers of the American business press need have no doubt of the importance of this factor. States take out large business advertisements to boast that they have the most favourable business climate, which usually means that they have the lowest taxes and weakest unions. Although – fortunately for the inhabitants of other states – many businesses are in favour of good educational systems, spending on the arts and other services, if only as factors attracting high-quality executives, such threats are an important long-term constraint. Liberal states within the USA, such as Wisconsin and Massachusetts, encounter major problems in trying to reconcile liberal policies on the environment, welfare, etc. with long-term economic growth. In contrast, in centralised systems the uniformity of regulations and laws throughout the nation ensures that businesses which are upset by the level of taxation or regulation must either seek redress by political action or take the extreme step of relocating in another country. National business organisations may thus be weaker in federal than in unitary systems because there are other ways to exert pressure.

Economic Factors

The nature of the economic structure of a country also influences the form of employers' representation. The most obvious potential influence is the degree of *industrial concentration*. Mancur Olson popularised amongst political scientists the problematic nature of interest group membership;[2] why should anyone, or any firm, join an interest group if they will profit by its successes whether or not they are members? It is plausible to suggest that this problem increases with the number of potential members of the group. In highly-concentrated economies, employers may thus be more likely to join interest groups than in less-concentrated economies in which the large number of employers will raise acutely the 'Olson problem'. At first sight this seems to be a plausible view. The less-concentrated, more competitive nature of the American economy might be seen as a reason for the slow and limited development of its employers' associations. In contrast, the more highly-concentrated economies such as Britain or Japan do indeed seem to have stronger employers' organisations. Yet the consequences of industrial concentration are more problematic than this suggests. The presence of very large firms may actually impede the creation of strong, authoritative employers' organisations, precisely because the large firm has the resources to make contact with government and to engage in lobbying itself. It is the smaller firm that needs the services of the employers' organisation. Dominant firms such as ICI have indeed been seen as one factor in Britain limiting the authority of trade associations: even though such firms support trade associations, they are large enough to talk directly to government.

A less obvious factor of some importance is the relationship between the *financial* institutions and *manufacturing* companies of a country. If, as in Britain, the two sectors are distinct, it will be difficult to create an organisation which will speak for both. British banks have in fact kept their distance from manufacturing companies, and from the interest groups such as the CBI which represent them. Indeed, the separation of financial and manufacturing interests in Britain has been a major constraint on the political power – as well as commercial success – of manufacturing companies. The absence of financial companies from the CBI weakened its authority, while the separate interests of the financial institutions were often more influential than the views of manufacturing industry. Partly in consequence, British governments have usually followed policies (such as on the exchange rate) which were much more advantageous to financial institutions than to manufacturers.

Three further economic factors have a considerable impact on the business–government relationship. The first is the degree to which an economy is involved in *international trade*. In economies which are extensively involved in international trade the capacity of governments to plan the economy is reduced. As the French and Japanese examples indicate, as economies become more involved in foreign trade, governments become less able to influence economic development, for both customers and suppliers are beyond their jurisdiction. It is striking that as the French economy became less self-contained and more involved in trade, the Five-year Plans, so much a feature of post-war France, became less and less meaningful. Similarly, the internationalising of the Japanese economy (or at least sales of Japanese goods) has diminished the leadership role of the Ministry of International Trade and Industry (MITI). Moreover, the need to achieve in the long term equilibrium in the balance of payments will make even a left-wing government attentive to the needs of major exporters or producers of import substitutes. Both the Mitterand Government in France and successive Labour Governments in Britain have been driven in part by such exigencies to listen very carefully to business.

A further economic factor of some significance is the degree to which government itself is the major *customer* of business. This is not quite the same as the question more commonly posed of the percentage of GNP to which government expenditures are equivalent. It is quite possible for a government's budget to be equivalent to a high percentage of the GNP without the government itself being a major customer. Transfer payments such as social security or old age pensions may simply shift money from one set of citizens to another, with government merely acting as the intermediary. On the other hand, government can also be a major customer, purchasing a high proportion of the output of the defence, aircraft and construction industries for its own use. To the degree that government itself is a major final consumer, individual firms will be 'politicised', realising that lobbying and political pressure are an inherent part of the company's life. Even while the organisations to defend the collective interests of American business were weak in the 1950s, individual firms seeking defence contracts were used to wage vigorous, often highly-visible contests for a contract to build a war plane. Defence contractors were aware that politics could be as important as design in winning a contract.

The final, and arguably most important, economic factor influencing the nature of business–government relations is the degree to which government engages in *economic planning*. If a country generally operates incomes policies, its government will have a compelling need to consult authoritative representatives of both unions and employers on the drafting and implementation of that policy. If governments decide that the economic performance of their economies would be improved by indicative planning, they will also need to strengthen the mechanisms for consulting employers. Planning also involves constant detailed dialogue between government and employers (and as in Austria or Sweden where they are strong enough, unions). Participation in planning will also change

the skills needed by an employers' organisation; political skills will
be less important than technocratic skills such as economic analysis
and forecasting. Planning thus encourages employers' organisations
to shift the balance in their staffs towards more technocratic
personnel as dealings between the government and employers'
organisation increasingly take the form of a constant dialogue in
which pressure, lobbying or campaigning seem either irrelevant, or
weapons to be used only as a last resort.

Does the Form of the Business–Government Relationship Matter?

It might of course be argued that these variations in the form of
the business–government relationship are not of great significance.
Marxists might argue that the variations which we have described
are surface phenomena, simply differences in the manner in which
the state maintains the capitalist mode of production – the state
takes on a variety of forms in order to contain, co-opt or repress
challenges to capitalism. Similarly, Lindblom's argument that business enjoys its privileged position fundamentally because of its
control over investment suggests that attention to the nature of
the institutional ties between business and government may be
misplaced.

Several answers might be given to such objections. First, the
variations in the form of the business–government relationship are
of interest and importance to scholars working in a variety of
traditions, including Marxism. Marxist scholars have moved away
from the quest for single theory of the state towards an awareness
that the forms of the relationship between capital, labour and the
state can differ significantly. Such variations can be explained in
Marxist terms by many factors which we have encountered above,
such as the balance of forces between the classes, and the degree to
which capital is fragmented or united. Though scholars in different
traditions might disagree on the nature and importance of factors
producing variations in the business–government relationship, few
would seriously deny the value of delineating such variations.

It is also clear that there are very marked differences between
countries in terms of their economic performance. The difference
between the Japanese and British economic growth rates in the last
decade, or between the Italian and German inflation rates or the

Swedish and Belgian unemployment rates has been more than four-fold. While it would be implausible to suggest that all the variations in the economic performance of countries can be explained by reference to their pattern of relationships between business, government and labour, it would be odd to suggest that these relationships had no impact either. How smoothly accommodations have been made between government, business and labour not only differs from country to country, but seems to have obvious consequences for economic success. Labour, for example, is sufficiently strong in both Britain and Austria to enjoy considerable power to inhibit or at least to limit business decisions. In Austria, that power has been used within consultative machinery that both reflects and promotes compromise. In Britain, such peaceful, long-term conflict resolution has been less frequent, with consequent economic losses through strikes and restrictive practices. In the USA, business has had few problems with unions since the 1940s, partly because of the labour relations legislation adopted then. However, the absence of machinery of compromise has been apparent in the difficulty in achieving agreement on effective but economically efficient regulations to protect the environment, workplace safety and health, or consumer protection. American business executives, though, spared the problem of dealing with British unions, would gladly exchange their own Environmental Protection Agency (EPA) for its British equivalent.

Towards Convergence?

It is striking that in all the countries we have surveyed business now faces a significant challenge to its interests. Even in the USA, so long thought of as the country where 'what was good for business was good for the country', and vice-versa, business has been confronted with the need to organise to defend itself from challenges from groups whose concerns, such as the environment, may have an adverse effect upon it. The old defences of business – deference, social prestige, the sympathy of all powerful politicians and the prevailing ideology – rarely seem to suffice these days. In spite of the talk in the 1970s of limits to growth, voters around the world remain attracted to economic expansion, a sentiment on which business can capitalise. Yet voters are also attracted to a range of policies which, through regulation or taxation, are likely to create problems for business. Past ages have been celebrated as ages of business organisation in which the giant corporation replaced the small-scale enterprise; the administered price replaced the fervent competition of an earlier age. Business round the world today, faced with numerous challenges to its concerns and interests, can rarely afford to neglect its political representation. In a sense, therefore, we are living in an age of business *political* organisation in which employers will routinely concern themselves (or employ others to concern themselves) with political issues which rarely troubled their predecessors. British business executives in the 1970s were much concerned by the need to improve the quality of British trade associations; simultaneously in the USA, business executives were moving to strengthen the organisations intended to protect their collective interests. Even in the countries in which business groups had been weak, the imperatives of the age of business political organisation were felt.

How far might such trends go? Would one expect to find more similarity between business in different countries in ten years' time in terms of the nature of the business organisations? Any attempt at an answer is bound to be tentative. It would seen improbable, however, that the trend towards the increased political organisation of business will result in the same forms of business political organisation in all countries. This is in part because the influences of political institutions on the forms of interest organisation are too strong, and in part because there is no uniformity in the political trends of the advanced industrial democracies. The late 1970s and early 1980s resulted in major changes in some of the countries we have covered, bringing to power radical right-wing régimes in Britain and the USA. In France, in contrast, the election of the first socialist government of the Fifth Republic took policy in a different direction, though the radicalism of the Mitterrand Government was soon restrained by economic trends. In yet other countries, such as Germany, Sweden, Austria and Japan, policy directions, and the ties between business and government, have changed much less. Neither the institutional settings nor the policy changes of the advanced industrial democracies would thus seem to be working towards uniformity in business's involvement in politics and government. The observer in twenty years' time will be struck by the diversity, as well as the extent, of the political and governmental ties of business in advanced industrial democracies.

Notes and References

1 Introduction

1. Adam Yarmolinsky, *The Military Establishment* (New York: Harper Colophon, 1971); Paul A. C. Koistiner, *The Military Industrial Complex, An Historical Perspective* (New York: Praeger, 1980)

2. Robert Engler, *The Politics of Oil, Private Power and Democratic Directions* (Chicago: University of Chicago Press, 1961); Peter Odell, *Oil and World Power* (Harmondsworth: Pelican Books, 1981); Robert Engler, *The Brotherhood of Oil* (Chicago: University of Chicago Press, 1977).

3. Ralph Miliband, *The State in Capitalist Society* (London: Quartet Books, 1976); C. Wright Mills, *The Power Elite* (New York: Oxford University Press, 1956).

4. Elizabeth Drew, *Politics and Money, The New Road to Corruption* (New York: Macmillan, 1983).

5. See Miliband, *The State in Capitalist Society*; Mills, *The Power Elite*.

6. For an attempt to construct such a theory from fragments available, see Ralph Dahrendorf, *Class and Class Conflict in Industrial Society* (Stanford: Stanford University Press, 1959).

7. Robert Dahl, *Who Governs?* (New Haven, Conn.: Yale University Press, 1961).

8. Peter Bachrach and Morton Baratz, 'The Two Faces of Power', *American Political Science Review*, 56 (1962) pp. 947–52.

9. Matthew Crenson, *The Un-Politics of Air Pollution, A Study of Non-Decisionmaking in American Cities* (Baltimore and London: Johns Hopkins Press, 1972).

10. Steven Lukes, *Power, A Radical View* (London: Macmillan, 1964).

11. Charles E. Lindblom, *Politics and Markets, The World's Political Economic Systems* (New York: Basic Books, 1977).

12. Werner Sombart, *Why Is There No Socialism in the United States?* (London: Macmillan, 1976).

13. Raymond Bauer, Ithiel de Sola Pool and Lewis Anthony Dexter, *American Business and Public Policy* (Chicago: Aldine, 1972).

14. Theodore Lowi, 'American Business, Public Policy Case Studies and Political Theory', *World Politics*, 16, no. 4 (July 1964) pp. 677–715.

15. Philippe Schmitter has been the leading figure in such discussions. See his 'Still the Century of Corporatism?' *Review of Politics*, 36. no. 1 (January 1974) pp. 85–131; 'Modes of Interest Intermediation and Models of Social Change in Western Europe', *Comparative Political Studies*, 10, no. 1 (1977) pp. 7–38; Gerhard Lehmbruch and Philippe Schmitter (eds), *Patterns of Corporatist Policymaking* (London: Sage, 1982).

16. E. E. Schattschneider argued – quite plausibly – that the Republican Party was business's chief power resource in the USA. See his book *The Semi-Sovereign People, A Realist's View of Democracy in the United States* (New York: Holt, Rinehart & Winston, 1960).

17. See Barrington Moore, *The Social Origins of Dictatorship and Democracy* (London: Allen Lane, The Penguin Press, 1967).

18. Chalmers Johnson, *MITI and the Japanese Miracle, The Growth of Industrial Policy 1925–75* (Stanford: Stanford University Press, 1982).

19. See, for example, James Wilson's introduction to Steven Kelman's book *Regulating America, Regulating Sweden, A Comparative Study of Occupational Safety and Health Policy* (Cambridge, Mass.: MIT Press, 1981).

2 Business and Politics in the USA

1. See *Public Opinion*, June–July 1980.

2. Andrew Shonfield, *Modern Capitalism, The Changing Balance of Public and Private Power* (Oxford: Oxford University Press, 1969).

3. Anthony King, 'Ideas, Institutions and the Policies of Governments', *British Journal of Political Science*, 3 (July 1973) pp. 291–313.

4. Louis Hartz, *The Liberal Tradition in America* (New York: Harcourt, Brace & World, 1955).

5. Seymour Martin Lipset, 'Why No Socialism in the United States?', in Seweryn Bialer and Sophia Sluzar (eds), *Sources of Contemporary Radicalism, Vol. I* (Boulder, Colo.: Westview Press, 1977) pp. 31–150.

6. For a short history of unions in the USA, see G. K. Wilson, *Unions in American National Politics* (London: Macmillan, 1979).

7. See *Public Opinion*, June–July 1980.

8. See James Q. Wilson (ed.), *The Politics of Regulation* (New York: Basic Books, 1980); Steven Kelman, *Regulating America, Regulating Sweden, A Comparative Study of Occupational Safety and Health Policy* (Cambridge, Mass.: MIT Press, 1981); David Vogel, 'Co-Operative Regulation; Environmental Protection in Britain', *Public Interest*, 72 (Summer 1983) pp. 88–106.

9. Richard Gable, 'NAM: Influential Lobby or Kiss of Death?', *Journal of Politics*, 15, no. 2 (May 1953) pp. 254–73.

10. Raymond Bauer, Ithiel de Sola Pool and Lewis Anthony Dexter, *American Business and Public Policy* (Chicago: Aldine, 1972).

11. For amplification of the argument which follows, see G. K. Wilson, *Interest Groups in the United States* (Oxford: Oxford University Press, 1981); and David Vogel, 'The Power of Business in the United States, A Reappraisal', *British Journal of Political Science*, 13 (1983) pp. 19–43.

12. E. E. Schattschneider, *The Semi-Sovereign People, A Realist's View of Democracy in the United States* (New York: Holt, Rinehart & Winston, 1960).

13. See G. William Domhoff, *Who Rules America?* (Englewood Cliffs, N J: Prentice-Hall, 1967).

14. For an attack on the possibility of an industrial policy, see Amitai Etzioni, *Public Interest*, 72 (1983) pp. 44–51. For a more balanced discussion, see Robert B. Reich, 'An Industrial Policy of the Right', *Public Interest*, 73 (1983) pp. 3–18.
15. Marver Bernstein, *Regulating Business by Independent Commission* (Princeton, N J: Princeton University Press, 1955).
16. See Wilson (ed.), *The Politics of Regulation*; Kelman, *Regulating America*; Eugene Bardach and Robert Kagan, *Going by the Book, Unreasonableness in Protective Regulation* (Philadelphia: Temple University Press, 1981).
17. The major works in this debate are Robert Dahl, *Who Governs?* (New Haven, Conn.: Yale University Press, 1961); Matthew Crenson, *The Un-Politics of Air Pollution, A Study of Non-Decisionmaking in American Cities* (Baltimore and London: John Hopkins Press, 1972).
18. For a most helpful discussion, see Tina Rosenberg, 'Why Tax Incentives Are a Bad Idea for the States', *New Republic*, 3 October 1983, pp. 18–21. Marxists, too, show an awareness that business has interests other than the lowest possible rate of taxation. See James O'Connor, *The Fiscal Crisis of the State* (New York: St Martin's Press, 1973).

3 Business and Politics in West Germany

1. Eric Owen Smith, *The West German Economy* (London and Canberra: Croom Helm, 1983) p.10.
2. Ibid., p. 13.
3. Graham Hallett, *The Social Market Economy of West Germany* (London: Macmillan, 1976).
4. Herbert Schatz, 'The Development of Political Planning in the Federal Republic of West Germany', in Klaus von Beyme (ed.), *German Political Systems* (London: Sage, 1976) p. 48.
5. For the early history of the BDI, see Gerard Braunthal, *The Federation of German Industry in Politics* (Ithaca, NY: Cornell University Press, 1965).

4 Business and Politics in Britain

1. Richard Rose, 'Two and One Half Cheers for Capitalism', *Public Opinion*, 6, no. 3 (June–July 1983) pp. 10–15.
2. For comparison between the advanced industrialised democracies in these respects, see Anthony King, 'Ideas, Institutions and the Policies of Governments', *British Journal of Political Science*, 3 (July 1973) pp. 291–313.
3. This conclusion was reached by a comparison of productivity in car factories conducted by the Central Policy Review staff. The study is criticised in Karel Williams, John Williams and Denis Thomas, *Why Are the British Bad at Manufacturing?* (London: Routledge & Kegan Paul, 1983), who argue that British wages are so low that poor productivity does not matter; British workers are paid less for producing less. This is scarcely comforting.

144 *Notes and References*

4. Perhaps the most interesting attempt to explain this is Martin Wiener's *English Culture and the Decline of the Industrial Spirit, 1850–1980* (Cambridge, Mass.: Cambridge University Press, 1981).
5. Michael Moran, *The Politics of Industrial Relations* (London: Macmillan, 1977).
6. Michael Pinto-Duchinsky, 'Financing the British Election of 1979', in A. Ranney (ed.), *Britain at the Polls* (Washington, DC: American Enterprise Institute, 1979).
7. The major work on the CBI is Wyn Grant and David Marsh, *The Confederation of British Industries* (London: Hodder & Stoughton, 1977). See also Marsh in David Marsh (ed.), *Pressure Politics, Interest Groups in Britain* (London: Junction Books, 1983).
8. Frank Longstreth, 'The City, Industry and the State', in Colin Crouch (ed.), *State and Economy in Contemporary Capitalism* (London: Croom Helm, 1979); D. Marsh and G. Locksley, 'Capital, the Neglected Face of Power?', in Marsh (ed.), *Pressure Politics*, pp. 21–52.
9. Michael Moran, 'Finance Capital and Pressure Group Politics in Britain', *British Journal of Political Science*, 11, part 4 (October 1981) pp. 381–404.
10. Committee to Review the Functioning of Financial Institutions (Sir Harold Wilson, Chairman) *Report* (London: HMSO, 1980, Cmnd 7937).
11. Commission of Enquiry into Industrial and Commercial Representation (Lord Devlin, Chairman) *Report* (London: Association of British Chambers of Commerce/Confederation of British Industries, 1972).
12. Raymond Bauer, Ithiel de Sola Pool and Lewis Anthony Dexter, *American Business and Public Policy* (Chicago: Aldine, 1972).
13. For a vigorous attack on this process, see S. E. Finer, *Adversary Politics and Electoral Reform* (London: Anthony Wigram, 1975).
14. On this, see Douglas Ashford, *Policy and Politics in Britain, The Limits of Consensus* (Oxford: Basil Blackwell, 1981).

5 Government and Industry in France

1. Laurence Wylie, *Village in the Vaucluse* (Cambridge, Mass.: Harvard University Press, 1957).
2. The study is quoted by Suleiman in Steven J. Warnecke and Ezra N. Suleiman (eds), *Industrial Policies in Western Europe* (New York: Praeger, 1975) p. 25.
3. Alexis de Tocqueville, *The Old Regime and the French Revolution* (Garden City, NY: Doubleday, 1955).
4. Jack Hayward, 'Employer Associations and the State in France and Britain' in Warnecke and Suleiman (eds), *Industrial Policies*, pp. 137–8.
5. Ibid., p. 137.
6. John Zysman, *Political Strategies for Industrial Order, State Market and Industry in France* (Berkeley: University of California Press, 1977) p. 63.
7. Henry Ehrman, 'An Exchange Theory of Interest Groups', in R. H. Salisbury (ed.), *Interest Groups in America* (New York: Harper & Row, 1977) pp. 43–5.
8. Hayward, *Employer Associations*, p. 130.

9. Frank L. Wilson, 'Alternative Models of Interest Intermediation: The Case of France', *British Journal of Political Science*, 12, part 2 (April 1982) p. 189.
10. Zysman, *Political Strategies*, p. 63.
11. Hayward, *Employer Associations*, p. 129.
12. See Diane Green, 'The Seventh Plan; The Demise of French Planning?' *West European Politics*, 1 (February 1978) pp. 60–76.
13. For the definitive study, see J. H. MacArthur and B. R. Scott, *Industrial Planning in France* (Cambridge, Mass.: Harvard University Press, 1969).
14. Andrew Shonfield, *Modern Capitalism, The Changing Balance of Public and Private Power* (Oxford: Oxford University Press, 1969) pp. 130–1.
15. MacArthur and Scott, *Industrial Planning*, p. 8.
16. Stephen Cohen, *Modern Capitalist Planning, The French Model* (Cambridge, Mass.: Harvard University Press, 1969) p. 51.
17. Quoted in Anthony King, 'Ideas, Institutions and the Policies of Governments,' *British Journal of Political Science*, 3 (1973) pp. 291–313.
18. Stanley Hoffman, 'The State: For What Society?' in Stanley Hoffman (ed.), *Decline or Renewal? France Since the 1930s* (New York: Viking Press, 1974) p. 450.
19. Anne Stevens, 'The Higher Civil Service and Economic Policy-Making', in Philip G. Cerny and Martin A. Schain (eds), *French Politics and Public Policy* (London and New York: Methuen, 1981).
20. Vincent Wright, *The Government and Politics of France* (London: Hutchinson, 1973) p. 90.
21. Suleiman, in Warnecke and Suleiman (eds), *Industrial Policies*, p. 37.
22. Charles Kindelberger, 'The Postwar Resurgence of the French Economy', in Stanley Hoffman (ed.), *In Search of France* (New York: Harper Torch Books, 1967) pp. 118–158.

6 Japan Inc.?

1. For a paean of praise for the Japanese achievement, see Ezra Vogel, *Japan as Number One, Lessons for America* (New York: Harper Colophon, 1982).
2. An indispensable guide to the evolution of industrial policy in Japan is Chalmers Johnson, *MITI and the Japanese Miracle, The Growth of Industrial Policy, 1925–75* (Stanford: Stanford University Press, 1982).
3. A most useful discussion of this question can be found in US Department of Commerce, *Japan: The Business–Government Relationship* (Washington, DC: Government Printing Office, 1974).
4. For a discussion of the reasons why, see J. A. Stockwin, *Japan; Divided Politics in a Growth Society*, 2nd ed (London: Weidenfeld & Nicholson, 1982) pp. 163–96.
5. For a brief description, see Stockwin, *Japan* pp. 115–36.
6. This argument is developed fully in Johnson, *MITI*.
7. T. J. Pempel and Keiich Tsunekawa, 'Corporatism without Labour' in Philippe C. Schmitter and Gerhard Lehmbruch (eds), *Trends Toward Corporatist Intermediation* (London and Beverly Hills: Sage, 1979) pp. 231–70.

7   The Neo-corporatist Nations

1.   For an argument that neo-corporatist countries are more governable, see Philippe Schmitter, 'Interest Intermediation and Regime Governability in Western Europe and North America', in Suzanne Berger (ed.), *Organising Interests in Western Europe; Pluralism and the Transformation of Politics* (Cambridge, Mass.: Cambridge University Press, 1981).
2.   The major article is again by Schmitter, 'Still the Century of Corporatism?', *Review of Politics*, 36, no. 1 (January 1974) pp. 85–131.
3.   The term 'liberal corporatism' is used by Gerhard Lehmbruch, 'Consociational Democracy, Class Conflict and the New Corporatism', in Philippe Schmitter and Gerhard Lehmbruch (eds), *Trends Toward Corporatist Intermediation* (London: Sage, 1979) pp. 53–62.
4.   Robert B. Kvavik, *Interest Groups in Norwegian Politics* (Oslo: Universitetsførlaget, 1976).
5.   For helpful summaries, see the chapters by Maria Szecsi, Felix Butschek and Peter Gerlich in Kurt Steiner (ed.), *Modern Austria* (Palo Alto, CA: Society for the Promotion of Science and Scholarship, 1981).
6.   M. Donald Hancock, *Sweden, The Politics of Post-Industrial Change* (London and New York: Holt, Rinehart & Winston, 1972).
7.   Samuel Beer, *Modern British Politics* (Cambridge, Mass.: Harvard University Press, 1965).
8.   See Schmitter, 'Interest Intermediation and Regime Governability'.
9.   Steven Kelman, *Regulating America, Regulating Sweden; A Comparative Study of Occupational Safety and Health Policy* (Cambridge, Mass.: MIT Press, 1981).

8   The Multinationals – Companies Without Governments?

1.   Much of the evidence is summarised conveniently in Anthony Sampson, *The Sovereign State of IT&T* (New York: Stein & Day, 1973).
2.   The evidence is contained in US Senate, Subcommittee on Multinational Corporations of the Committee on Foreign Relations, 93rd Congress, *The International Telephone and Telegraph Company and Chile, 1970–71*; US Senate, Committee to Study Government Operations with Respect to Intelligence Activities, Staff Report, *Covert Operations in Chile* (Washington, DC: Government Printing Office, 1975).
3.   Quoted in Charles E. Kindleberger (ed.), *The International Corporation* (Cambridge, Mass.: MIT Press, 1970) p. 320.
4.   G. Modelski, 'International Context and Performance Amongst the World's Largest Corporations', in G. Modelski (ed.), *Transnational Corporations and World Order* (San Francisco: Freeman, 1979).
5.   Raymond Vernon, *Storm over Multinationals, The Real Issues* (London: Macmillan, 1977).
6.   For an example of such research, see D. K. Fieldhouse *Unilever Overseas, The Anatomy of a Multinational, 1895–1965* (London: Croom Helm, 1978).

9 Conclusions

1. Samuel Beer, *Modern British Politics* (Cambridge, Mass.: Harvard University Press, 1965).
2. Mancur Olson, *The Logic of Collective Action* (Cambridge, Mass.: Harvard University Press, 1965).

Bibliography

Ashford, Douglas *Policy and Politics in Britain, The Limits of Consensus* (Oxford: Basil Blackwell, 1981).

Bachrach, Peter, and Morton Baratz, 'The Two Faces of Power', *American Political Science Review*, 56 (1962) pp. 947–532.

Bardach, Eugene, and Robert Kagan, *Going by the Book, Unreasonableness in Protective Regulation* (Philadelphia: Temple University Press, 1981).

Bauer, Raymond, Ithiel de Sola Pool and Lewis Anthony Dexter, *American Business and Public Policy* (Chicago: Aldine, 1972).

Beer, Samuel, *Modern British Politics* (Cambridge, Mass.: Harvard University Press, 1965).

Berger, Suzanne (ed.), *Organising Interests in Western Europe; Pluralism and the Transformation of Politics* (Cambridge, Mass.: Cambridge University Press, 1981).

Bernstein, Marver, *Regulating Business by Independent Commission* (Princeton, NJ: Princeton University Press, 1955).

Beyme, Klaus von (ed.), *German Political Systems* (London: Sage, 1976).

Braunthal, Gerard, *The Federation of German Industry in Politics* (Ithaca, N.Y.: Cornell University Press, 1965)

Cerny, Philip G. and Martin A. Schain (eds.) *French Politics and Public Policy*, (London: Methuen).

Cohen, Stephen, *Modern Capitalist Planning, The French Model* (Cambridge, Mass.: Harvard University Press, 1969).

Crenson, Matthew, *The Un-Politics of Air Pollution, A Study of Non-Decisionmaking in American Cities* (Baltimore and London: Johns Hopkins Press, 1972).

Crouch, Colin (ed.), *State and Economy in Contemporary Capitalism* (London: Croom Helm, 1979).

Dahl, Robert, *Who Governs?* (New Haven, Conn.: Yale University Press, 1961).

Devlin, Lord (Chairman), Committee of Enquiry into Industrial and Commerical Representation, *Report* (London: Association of British Chambers of Commerce, Confederation of British Industries, 1972).

Domhoff, G. William, *Who Rules America?* (Englewood Cliffs, NJ: Prentice-Hall, 1967).

Drew, Elizabeth, *Politics and Money, The New Road to Corruption* (New York; Macmillan, 1983).

Engler, Robert, *The Brotherhood of Oil* (Chicago: Unversity of Chicago Press, 1977).

____, *The Politics of Oil, Private Power and Democratic Directions* (Chicago: University of Chicago Press, 1961).

Fieldhouse, D. K., *Unilever Overseas, The Anatomy of a Multinational, 1895–1965* (London: Croom Helm, 1978).

Frank, Isaiah, *Foreign Enterprises in Developing Countries* (Baltimore and London: Johns Hopkins University Press, 1980).

Gable, Richard, 'NAM: Influential Lobby or Kiss of Death?' *Journal of Politics*, 15, no. 2 (May 1953) pp. 254–73.

Grant, Wyn, and David Marsh, *The Confederation of British Industries* (London: Hodder & Stoughton, 1977).

Green, Diane, 'The Seventh Plan; The Demise of French Planning?', *West European Politics*, 1 (February 1978) pp. 60–76.

Hallett, Graham, *The Social Market Economy of West Germany* (London: Macmillan, 1976).

Hancock, M. Donald, *Sweden, The Politics of Post-Industrial Change* (London and New York: Holt, Rinehart & Winston, 1972).

Hartz, Louis, *The Liberal Tradition in America* (New York: Harcourt, Brace & World, 1955).

Hoffman, Stanley (ed.), *Decline or Renewal? France Since the 1930s* (New York: Viking Press, 1974).

Johnson, Chalmers, *MITI and the Japanese Miracle, The Growth of Industrial Policy, 1925–75* (Stanford: Stanford University Press, 1982).

Johnson, Chalmers (ed.), *The Industrial Policy Debate* (San Francisco: ICS Press, 1984).

Kelman, Steven, *Regulating America, Regulating Sweden, A Comparative Study of Occupational Safety and Health Policy* (Cambridge, Mass.: MIT Press, 1981).

Kindelberger, Charles E. (ed.), *The International Corporation* (Cambridge, Mass.: MIT Press, 1970).

King, Anthony, 'Ideas, Institutions and the Policies of Governments', *British Journal of Political Science*, 3 (July 1973) pp. 291–313.

Koistiner, Paul A. C., *The Military Industrial Complex, An Historical Perspective* (New York: Praeger, 1980).

Kvavik, Robert B., *Interest Groups in Norwegian Politics* (Oslo: Universitetsførlaget, 1976).

Lehmbruch, Gerhard, and Phillippe Schmitter (eds), *Patterns of Corporatist Policymaking* (London: Sage 1982).

Lindbolm, Charles E., *Politics and Markets, The World's Political Economic Systems* (New York: Basic Books, 1977).

Lipset, Seymour Martin, 'Why No Socialism in the United States?' in Seweryn Bialer and Sophia Sluzar (eds), *Sources of Contemporary Radicalism, Vol. I* (Boulder, Colo.: Westview Press, 1977) pp. 31–150.

Longstreth, Frank, 'The City, Industry and the State', in Colin Crouch (ed.), *State and Economy in Contemporary Capitalism* (London: Croom Helm, 1979).

Lowi, Theodore, 'American Business, Public Policy Case Studies and Political Theory', *World Politics*, 16, no. 4 (July 1964) pp 677–715.

Lukes, Steven, *Power, A Radical View* (London: Macmillan, 1964).

MacArthur, J. H., and B. R. Scott, *Industrial Planning in France* (Cambridge, Mass.: Harvard University Press, 1969).

Marsh, David (ed.), *Pressure Politics, Interest Groups in Britain* (London: Junction Books, 1983).

Miliband, Ralph, *The State in Capitalist Society* (London: Quartet Books, 1976).

Mills, C. Wright, *The Power Elite* (New York: Oxford University Press, 1956).

Modelski, G. (ed.), *Transnational Corporations and World Order* (San Francisco: Freeman, 1979).

Moore, Barrington, *The Social Origins of Dictatorship and Democracy* (London: Allen Lane, The Penguin Press, 1967).

Moran, Michael, *The Politics of Industrial Relations* (London: Macmillan, 1977).

____, 'Finance Capital and Pressure Group Politics in Britain', *British Journal of Political Science*, 11, part 4 (October 1981) pp. 381–404.

O'Connor, James, *The Fiscal Crisis of the State* (New York: St Martins Press, 1973).

Pinto-Duchinsky, Michael, 'Financing the British General Election of 1979' in A. Ranney (ed.), *Britain at the Polls* (Washington, DC: American Enterprise Institute, 1979).

Rose, Richard, 'Two and One Half Cheers for Capitalism', *Public Opinion*, 6, no. 3 (June–July 1983) pp. 10–15.

Rosenberg, Tina, 'Why Tax Incentives Are a Bad Idea for the States', *New Republic*, 3 October 1983, pp. 18–21.

Salisbury, R. H. (ed.), *Interest Groups in America* (New York: Harper & Row).

Sampson, Anthony, *The Soverign State of IT&T* (New York: Stein & Day 1973).

Schnattschneider E. E., *The Semi-Sovereign People, A Realist's View of Democracy in the United States* (New York: Holt, Rinehart & Winston, 1960).

Schmitter, Philippe, 'Modes of Interest Intermediation and Models of Social Change in Western Europe', *Comparative Political Studies*, 10, no. 1 (1977) pp. 7–38.

____, 'Still the Century of Corporatism?' *Review of Politics*, 36, no. 1 (January 1974) pp. 85–131.

Schmitter, Philippe C. and Gerhard Lehmbruch (eds), *Trends Toward Corporatist Intermediation* (Beverly Hills: Sage, 1979).

Shonfield, Andrew, *Modern Capitalism, The Changing Balance of Public and Private Power* (Oxford: Oxford University Press, 1969).

Smith, Eric Owen, *The West German Economy* (London and Canberra: Croom Helm, 1983).

Sombart, Werner, *Why Is There No Socialism in the United States?* (London: Macmillan, 1976).

Stockwin, J. A., *Japan; Divided Politics in a Growth Society*, 2nd edn (London: Weidenfeld & Nicolson, 1982).

US Department of Commerce, *Japan; The Business–Government Relationship* (Washington, DC: Government Printing Office, 1974).

Vernon, Raymond, *Storm Over Multinationals, The Real Issues* (London: Macmillan, 1977).

Vogel, David, 'Co-operative Regulation; Environmental Protection in Britain', *Public Interest*, 72 (Summer 1983) pp. 88–106.

____, 'The Power of Business in the United States, A Re-appraisal', *British Journal of Political Science*, 13 (1983) pp. 19–43.

____, 'Why Businessmen Distrust Their State', *British Journal of Political Science*, 8, part 1 (January 1978) pp. 45–78.

Vogel, Erza, *Japan as Number One, Lessons for America* (New York: Harper Colophon, 1982).

Warnecke, Steven J., and Erza N. Suleiman (eds), *Industrial Policies in Western Europe* (New York: Praeger, 1975).

Wiener, Martin, *English Culture and the Decline of the Industrial Spirit, 1850–1980* (Cambridge, Mass.: Cambridge University Press, 1981).

Williams, Karel, John Williams and Denis Thomas, *Why are the British Bad at Manufacturing?* (London: Routledge & Kegan Paul, 1983).

Wilson, Frank, L., 'Alternative Models of Interest Intermediation: The Case of France', *British Journal of Political Science*, 12, part 2 (April 1982) pp. 173–200.

Wilson, G. K., *Unions in American National Politics* (London: Macmillan, 1979).

_____, *Interest Groups in the United States* (Oxford: Oxford University Press, 1981).

Wilson, Sir Harold (Chairman), Committee to Review the Functioning of Financial Institutions, *Report* (London: HMSO, 1980) Cmnd 7937).

Wilson, James Q. (ed.), *The Politics of Regulation* (New York: Basic Books, 1980).

Wright, Vincent, *The Government and Politics of France* (London: Hutchinson, 1975).

Yarmolinsky, Adam, *The Military Establishment* (New York: Harper Colophon, 1971).

Zysman, John, *Political Strategies for Industrial Order, State, Market and Industry in France* (Berkeley: University of California Press, 1977).

Index

National Farmers' Union (NFU) (of England and Wales) 20, 133
National Farmers' Union (of the USA) 20
National Labor Relations Board (NLRB) (of the USA) 29

Occupational Safety and Health Agency (of the USA) 26, 29, 31, 38
OGB (*Osterreicher Gewerk-schaftsbund*) (Austrian Trade Union Federation) 106
Olson, Mancur 135

PACs (Political Action Committees) *see* election campaign contributions by business
pantouflage 84, 91
parties, business links with
in Great Britain 60–1
in the USA 34
in West Germany 51–3
PCF (*French Communist Party*) 75, 76–7
planning
in France 21, 80–6
in Great Britain 68–74
in Japan 92, 100
in West Germany 49–50
pluralism
concept of 3–4
criticisms of 4–5
power, problems in defining 3–8
power elite 2–3
'privileged position' of business 6–7

regulation of business in the USA 26, 31, 38–40

Republican Party (of the USA) 14, 15
Roosevelt, President Franklin Delanor 25
Rose, Richard 57–8
Royal Dutch Shell 115

Schmitter, Philippe 111
Schneider, General 119
Scott, B. R. 82
Shapiro, Irving 34
Shonfield, Andrew 23, 26
Sierra Club (of the USA) 25
social market economy, in West Germany 44–8
Social Democratic Party (of Sweden) 103
Social Democratic Party (of West Germany) 49, 50, 50–1, 56
Sombart, Werner 7
Suleiman, Ezra 84–5

Talbot–Peugeot 83
Tokyo University 91
trade associations
in France 79–80
in Great Britain 66–8
in Japan 92–3
in the United States 30, 32–3
Trades Union Congress (of Great Britain) 18

UAW (United Auto Workers) (of the USA) 24
Unilever 115

Vernon, R. 126

Wilson, Charles 4